This isn't just another book about architecture. I'd have titled it "How to be a software architect." Goldman guides you on all aspects of the role, from making decisions that will impact a product for years to come to picking good names, taking aim at conventional wisdom along the way.

Daniel Jackson
Professor of Computer Science, MIT

Architects often struggle to have the intended impact within their organizations, despite having the necessary domain expertise and generating good ideas. Oliver's book offers key insights and pragmatic advice for individual architects and architecture teams—helping them to deliver successful outcomes in real world scenarios.

Dan Foygel
Senior Principal Architect, Adobe

Effective Software Architecture hits home with the most meaningful aspects of delivering software at scale. The considerations, concepts, and approaches described apply to everyone I've worked with, not just architecture teams. Oliver offers insights that are well written and immediately useful in both theory and practice.

Noah Edelstein
VP of Product Management, Smartsheet

The most frustrating projects in my career have been updating systems where the initial architecture grew without deliberation or documentation. Oliver Goldman's *Effective Software Architecture* dives into why thinking clearly about software architecture is so important and offers tools to do so. I wish everybody thought so deeply about architecture!

Andrew Certain
Distinguished Engineer, Amazon Web Services

T0293051

Effective Software
Architecture

Effective Software Architecture

Building Better Software Faster

Oliver Goldman

✦ Addison-Wesley

Cover Credit: ArtHead/Shutterstock

For information about buying this title in bulk quantities, or for special sales opportunities (which may include electronic versions; custom cover designs; and content particular to your business, training goals, marketing focus, or branding interests), please contact our corporate sales department at corpsales@pearsoned.com or (800) 382-3419.

For government sales inquiries, please contact governmentsales@pearsoned.com.

For questions about sales outside the U.S., please contact intlcs@pearson.com.

Visit us on the Web: informit.com/aw

Library of Congress Control Number: 2024934795

ISBN-13: 978-0-13-824932-8
ISBN-10: 0-13-824932-6

1 2024

To Gloria, for her love and partnership

Contents

Acknowledgments

This book contains the accumulation of knowledge and experience gained over decades of education and work. Far more people have influenced and informed those years than I can enumerate here. There are, however, some key players who should not go unmentioned.

I'll begin with my parents, Bernadine and Terry, and my siblings—Elizabeth, Leah, and Matthew. My parents purchased a Commodore 64 when I was nine and it's easy to trace my career in software back to its arrival in our family room. My childhood home was also full of books, thinking, and lots of word play. Somewhere in there I got the notion that I'd like to see my name on a book one day. Now the Commodore 64 has helped me realize that goal, too.

In high school, two excellent English teachers, Jeff Laing and Rick Thalman, taught me that I can write—and how to do it. I am forever grateful for their feedback and encouragement. And a big thank you to Tom Laeser, who gave me free reign in the computer lab.

At college, I was fortunate to have Mendel Rosenblum as my advisor, as well as the instructor for my operating system classes—those were my favorites. During the summers and for a time after college I also had the privilege of working for George Zweig. George put a lot of trust in a much younger, more impetuous version of me. To this day, I look back fondly at those early experiences.

I spent the bulk of my career at Adobe, with so many amazing colleagues that it's unfair to mention just a few and impossible to list them all. Nonetheless, I feel obliged to call out Winston Hendrickson and Abhay Parasnis as the two managers who gave me the biggest opportunities; I hope I have lived up to their expectations. Boris Prüßmann, Dan Foygel, Leonard Rosenthol, Roey Horns, and Stan Switzer were inspiring collaborators on all manner of projects, including the development and refinement of many of the ideas in this text.

Brett Adam, Dan Foygel, Kevin Stewart, and Roey Horns all reviewed early drafts of this book and provided valuable feedback. To Manjula Anaskar, Haze Humbert, Menka Mehta, Mary Roth, Jay-aprakash P., and others behind the scenes at Pearson: Thank you for taking a chance with a new author and your guidance along the way. You have helped me achieve one of my lifelong goals and I am deeply grateful.

Most of all, I want to thank my wife, Gloria, and our four boys. This book has been written from the comfort of the home we've made together and I wouldn't have it any other way.

About the Author

Oliver Goldman leads the AEC software architecture practice at Autodesk. He has thirty years of industry experience delivering innovative products in distributed real-time interaction, scientific computing, financial systems, mobile application development, and cloud architecture at Adobe and other employers. He holds two degrees in computer science from Stanford University, is an inventor on over 50 US software patents, and has previously contributed to *Dr. Dobb's Journal*.

Introduction

When I graduated from college with a degree in computer science, it's fair to say I had a layperson's understanding of the science and theory of creating software. I had studied databases, algorithms, compilers, graphics, CPU architecture, operating systems, concurrency, and more. And I had, to some extent, a framework that related these technologies to each other.

Because I was writing software outside of classes—mostly for summer jobs—I also knew that translating academic knowledge into building a product was a distinct challenge. More accurately, it presented challenges, plural. Selecting and implementing the right algorithm was generally the easy part. Working with a large code base, creating a functional user experience, testing for quality and performance, and coordinating with a whole team operating in parallel on the same product—these were hard things to do.

Upon graduation, I worked at a series of jobs developing software products. Most of them did not result in successful products, but that didn't stop me from learning from those experiences. If the cliches about learning from failure are correct, I learned a lot during that stretch of time.

Over the course of several different projects, I noticed that I often had a better view of the product as a system—that is, of the components within it and how they relate—than most of my peers. Although I didn't appreciate it at the time, this ability to see and reason about the "big picture" is a relatively rare but quite useful skill set.

To comprehensively address all the components of a software system and how they relate is to practice architecture. Obviously, the term *architecture* is not unique to software—indeed, it's borrowed from the realm of buildings, and can be applied to products of all types. Houses have an architecture, and so do cars, TVs, and rockets. Had I grown up to be a rocket scientist, I expect I'd have found myself more interested in how all the different parts of a rocket fit together than the design of a specific valve or nozzle. But we'll never know for sure, given that I ended up in the software field.

Over my decades in the industry, the complexity of the software we produce has grown immensely. When I started, a viable software product—that is, something that could be sold for a profit—fit on a floppy disk, ran on one machine at a time, and didn't connect to the Internet. Today, a software product running "in the cloud" might easily consist of hundreds of coordinating programs running at multiple, geographically distributed sites, updated multiple times a day, and expected to operate forever without interruption (an expectation of which we admittedly sometimes fall short). The nature of a software product has evolved radically in a short time.

This evolution has made software architecture both more difficult and more critical than ever. More difficult because there are orders of magnitude more components and relationships to keep track of. More critical because, unless these relationships are managed effectively, the complexity of a system will inevitably become a limiting factor on its dependability and the velocity of further development. For most products, this is the beginning of the end. And I've seen it happen.

Software architecture isn't just about managing complexity, but if I had to pick the most valuable outcome of architecture as a discipline, that would be it. Complexity undermines everything that software should do for us. It creates unpredictable behavior, and thus undermines user trust. It leads to defects, harming dependability. It propagates failures, turning small errors into large outages. And it hampers understanding, eventually defeating any attempt to return to a simpler state or structure. Complexity is software's enemy, and a disciplined architecture practice its best defense.

Later in my career, I had the privilege and responsibility of leading architecture teams for a couple of large, complex software products. Neither product was entirely new; both had been around for more than a decade. I began by doing the sorts of things that are part of any architect's job description: understanding the system's current architecture, assessing its suitability for the current and anticipated requirements, and proposing and evaluating changes. I'll have more to say about how to do these things later in the book.

Although those activities are clearly necessary, equating them with software architecture is like saying I knew how to write software because I'd taken some computer science classes. It's a great start, but there's a whole lot more to making software architecture an integral and successful part of software development. And that's what this book is about: how to practice architecture in a software development organization.

Focus

This is not a book of software architectures. There are no explanations of client–server, domain-driven design, sense–compute–control, and other architectural styles. I do not discuss how to select a database technology, regionalize your deployments, or design for scale. Those are all important topics. There are many books, blogs, and other resources about them; there are many architects well versed in these topics.

But just as knowing how to implement a merge sort algorithm falls short of what's required to write an application, simple familiarity with a given architecture is woefully inadequate to create a system that uses it. And while adopting that merge sort might be the scope of a task that falls to a single engineer, system architecture inevitably involves a larger cast of characters.

This book aims to describe how you can take your architectural skills and knowledge and apply them to the much larger, much messier process of developing a product. Without focusing on a specific style, it defines software architecture, placing it and defining its role among the other specializations of a product development team. It identifies the many touchpoints that architecture has with the concepts, processes, standards, and so on that surround it.

We then dive deeply into the topic of change. Identifying, managing, and designing changes to a system are core to architecture practice. Design sometimes seems like a black box, with conversations going in one side and a complete design popping out the other. In reality, the whole process of change is ongoing and consists of discrete steps.

Everything we can do to make those steps apparent, to make them visible, and to steward them along this path will improve the process.

Engineering is about trade-offs, and the process of developing and evolving a system through change involves an endless litany of design decisions. Each decision opens some pathways and closes others—or perhaps it reverses an earlier decision when we discover a path has come to a dead end. How these decisions are made is itself a key skill. The more good decisions a project team can make, the less time is spent backing up. And the more quickly good decisions can be made, the more quickly the project can move ahead.

On projects of any significant size, logistics and communication also become critical considerations. Which decisions have been made, and which ones are pending? What's the vocabulary we use to describe our system? Why did we select the architecture that we're using? All these become concerns of tools, process, and communication.

Finally, we consider the architecture team in an organizational context, including the definition of software architect as a discrete role. Options for structuring an architecture team are considered, as well as how architects should engage with other disciplines within the organization. This section also considers how to identify, nurture, and develop architectural talent.

Motivation

Software grows ever more complex. We've grown accustomed to products that put the information and tools we want to use at our fingertips across multiple devices, anywhere on the globe, while supporting billions of users. The challenges involved in creating and operating these systems are far beyond the simple, stand-alone software products of just a few decades ago.

Software architecture plays a unique and critical role in this work. While only one of many disciplines that work together to conceive, realize, and run these massive systems, it uniquely demands an ability to see the "big picture," to understand how all the elements of a system come together, and to evolve that structure over time. Over the last two decades or so, architects have made great strides in developing technologies and techniques to meet these challenges. The better an organization is at doing software architecture, the better it will be at delivering quality software on time.

Even so, most product development organizations are not as good at doing software architecture as they could be. This observation crystallized for me one day when I took on a new role running a team of experienced architects on a project that was new to me. At the individual level, these architects were all adept at handling the challenges of designing software. However, they weren't packaging their skills to benefit the larger effort. They were underinvested in documentation, process, and communication.

As a result, that architecture team was underperforming. They struggled to prioritize their work, and sometimes engaged with the wrong problems. Without a strong decision-making process, they struggled to make decisions—and to keep them made. They were inconsistent in documenting their work, which sometimes led to work being ignored or redone. The project was complex and important; it warranted a significant architectural investment. But the team, despite having, collectively, more than a hundred years of architectural experience, was letting the organization down.

When I spoke with the members of my new team, I realized that they could see the symptoms—they knew they were struggling—but they could not identify the cause. They knew, individually, how to do software architecture. But collectively, they did not understand how to run an effective software architecture practice. They lacked the structure necessary to knit their individual efforts into a team effort and to integrate that work into the larger organization.

That experience led directly to this book. If these architects, with their decades of experience, didn't understand how to structure an effective architectural practice, then it was likely that many others struggled with the same issues. And while the endeavor of running an architecture team is not entirely ignored in software literature, it is also not a topic with extensive coverage. For example, *Software Architecture: Foundations, Theory, and Practice* (Taylor, Medvidovic, and Dashofy 2010) devotes 3% of its 675 pages to "People, Roles, and

Teams." I have a reasonably extensive library of books on software architecture; this is about par for the course. I decided to fill that gap.

Audience

This book is for software architects, the managers who lead them, and their counterparts in product management, user experience, program management, and other related disciplines. Building software is a joint space in which all these disciplines cooperate. I hope they will all benefit from these explanations of software architecture as a discipline, its role in software development, and how architects and architecture teams operate.

Practicing architects will find guidance that they can compare to their own methods. No matter how numerous their years of experience, they may yet find something new here. Software architecture is too young a field to have a broadly known corpus and consistent or regulated practice.

This book is also for everyone who works with a software architecture team. As projects expand, roles become differentiated: Product managers focus on requirements, testing teams create test plans, security teams develop threat models. Everyone has their own area of expertise. And yet all of those activities must be stitched back together into a cohesive whole—and that requires that everyone see how these functions fit together. In short, they must understand the system's architecture. In this book, everyone involved in software projects will find an accessible description of the role software architecture plays in achieving their goals.

Finally, this book is for the executives responsible for managing or creating an architecture team. In explaining how software architecture works, it provides the background that executives need to determine if their current architectural function is fit-for-purpose and what to look for when hiring new talent.

Success

An effective software architecture function helps product development organizations produce better software faster. As a discipline, software architecture tackles some of the hardest parts of producing software: organizing each system, managing change and complexity, designing for efficiency and dependability. Software systems with good architecture work well and continue to work well over time. Systems with poor architecture fail—often in spectacular fashion.

A successful software architecture practice also integrates these abilities with the broader challenges of product development. Architects are uniquely positioned to aggregate requirements, and thus design a cohesive whole instead of a collection of parts. And thanks to that same overarching view, they are also well positioned to communicate to everyone how those pieces come together.

To do that well requires more than a degree in computer science, and more than experience with relevant architectural styles. It requires the ability to create a predictable, repeatable change process; to make decisions expediently and effectively; and to build a team that can do these things ever better over time.

Simply put, software architecture has an ever-increasing impact on our ability to develop and deliver fit-for-purpose software. I hope this book will help guide you and your organization to a more effective software architecture practice.

Register your copy of **Effective Software Architecture: Building Better Software Faster** on the InformIT site for convenient access to updates and/or corrections as they become available. To start the registration process, go to informit.com/register and log in or create an account. Enter the product ISBN (**9780138249328**) and click Submit.

Chapter 1
Software Architecture

An effective software architecture practice helps product development organizations produce better software faster. But before we can discuss an effective practice, we need an understanding of software architecture. It's a term that's used frequently in the software industry, and often with a certain laxness. Tightening up our definition is important, as the practices in this book are closely aligned with a strict and complete definition of architecture.

Software architecture is often equated with software design, but the two are actually quite distinct. A *design* is a specific, point-in-time arrangement of software components that, collectively, form a software system. As we develop each release of that system and determine how that release will function, we are *designing* that release.

What happens when we create the next iteration of that same system? We'll revise its design, of course: That's how we introduce the changes that distinguish one release from the next. But we won't throw it out and start over, either; each subsequent design is related to the one that came before.

An *architecture* is a template for the iterative creation of a set of related designs. Architectures are also designed, but they are more than *a design*. Thus, an effective software architecture practice doesn't just create one good design; it lays the foundation for creating tens, hundreds, and thousands of designs. That's the potential of software architecture, and that's the promise of an effective software architecture practice.

What, then, constitutes an architecture? Standards play an important part in architecture, so it feels appropriate to start our discussion of architecture with a definition from an IEEE standard:

> *[An architecture is] the fundamental organization of a system, embodied in its components, their relationships to each other and the environment, and the principles governing its design and evolution. [1]*

Let's take this definition apart, piece by piece, to understand it thoroughly.

Fundamental Organization

Imagine that you have a software product consisting of a hundred components. The precise nature of these components doesn't matter; they could be services, libraries, containers, functions, or plugins. The point is that your product is composed of these components, and the interactions between these components realize the features and functions of the product.

Now imagine that for each component, you used a random number generator to determine its type (service, library, etc.) and its method of communication. Often these are linked—for example, a code library is designed to be invoked via a local procedure call, and a service is not. That's okay; we'll pick, randomly, from the methods that reasonably apply to each component.

You've probably already realized that getting these components to work together will be a challenge. Different components require different implementation technologies, tooling, and deployment.

We'll have lots of mismatches when we try to wire components up, and we'll have to translate between local calls and remote calls and message-passing and function invocation. In starting with randomness, we've constructed a system that lacks any fundamental organization. Fortunately, this system exists only in our imagination.

No one works this way, and every real system has some fundamental organization to it. The fundamental organization of a system often is, to some extent, imposed by external factors. For example, if you're building a mobile application, your elements will primarily be libraries and they'll mostly communicate via local procedure calls. In contrast, if you're building a cloud-based product, you might organize your system around services.

When speaking of the architecture of a system, however, we are generally referring to a fundamental organization that goes beyond these external constraints. For example, cloud services necessarily communicate via the network. Is that communication organized as request-response or message-passing? Any system that chooses one method over the other is fundamentally organized around that specific approach.

Figure 1.1 illustrates the impact of each approach to establishing a system's fundamental organization. As illustrated in the leftmost diagram, a randomized system consists of different types of components (indicated by different shapes) communicating via different mechanisms (indicated by different line types), and with arbitrary relationships. External constraints tend to dictate component types and communication mechanisms, as indicated by the uniformity of shapes and line types in the middle diagram. However, external constraints rarely impose organization on relationships within the system. The final diagram, on the right side of Figure 1.1, illustrates a system with a clear fundamental organization. It uses a consistent component type, consistent communication mechanism, and has structured relationships.

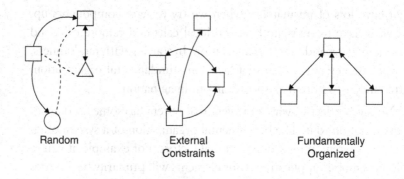

Random   External Constraints   Fundamentally Organized

Of a System

We're going to use the word "system" a lot in this book. The term appears in our definition of architecture and has already been mentioned half a dozen times in this chapter. But what is a system?

For our purposes, a *system* is any set of software components that work together to provide one or more capabilities. Systems can be large: They might contain hundreds or thousands of components and execute on a similar number of computers. But they can also be small: The embedded software running on a battery-powered wireless sensor is also a system.

Systems need not work in isolation. If you are developing wireless sensor software, then, for your purposes, the boundaries of your system can be set according to which software runs on the sensor. That sensor—along with others—will send data to some *other* system that processes that data. For you, the processing system may form part of your environment, not your system; it may, for example, be developed by a different team.

Systems may also be composed of other systems. In other words, a new system can be defined as the composition of two or more smaller systems, perhaps with some additional components added to the mix. For example, a system of wireless sensors, combined with a system for data processing, can be composed into a single system providing a monitoring capability.

Thus, when we use the term *system* regarding architecture, we're allowing for the system boundaries to be set as befits the relevant scope of concern. Every aspect of software architecture covered by this book applies to any of these systems, regardless of its scale. Granted, some concerns are more readily addressed at smaller scales, so the extent and rigor with which you apply architectural practice can be adjusted according to the needs of the system at hand.

Embodied in Its Components

The fundamental organization of a system isn't easy to change. The implied decisions regarding technology, communication, structure, and so on become embodied in the components that conform to that organization. After all, it's the implementation of this organization in the components that gives the whole system form.

It is all too easy to underestimate how deep these decisions run. As desktop computing gave way to mobile- and cloud-based solutions, companies with deep investments in desktop code looked for options to bring their massive investments in these code bases into these new forms.

Initially, that challenge might have looked like a porting problem. Maybe the code needed to run on a new CPU architecture or adapt to a different operating system. Those changes are not necessarily easy to make, but they're not impossible. Furthermore, many of these code bases had already been through at least one similar port in the past, such as from Windows to macOS.

But the fundamental organization of most desktop applications includes much more than just a CPU instruction set or even an operating system. For example, most of these desktop applications are organized around the assumption that they have access to a fast, reliable, local disk. This point is so foundational that many desktop application architects wouldn't have even called it out. There was no other option to consider; it could go unstated.

As a result, in many of these applications, the assumption of fast and reliable access to a disk is embodied not just in every component but in every line of code in those components. Need to read some configuration data? User preferences? Save progress? No problem! A couple of calls to the filesystem API, problem solved.

Moving this data to the cloud breaks this assumption, and every line of code that depends on it. The data might exist, but retrieving it might be slow (because it's over the network) and unreliable (because it's over the network). Or it might be impossible right now (because the network is down), although later it will be possible again.

Figure 1.2 illustrates how these assumptions become embodied in a system's components. On the left, components in a desktop application connect directly and independently to a file system; they assume and depend on fast and immediate access to their data.

Figure 1.2

The fundamental organization of a system is embodied in its components. On the left, the organization of the system around a file system is embodied in every component. On the right, that's been shifted to a cache that mediates access to data.

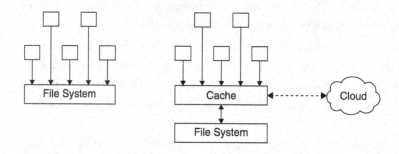

Components can be written to deal with this uncertainty, but they must embody a different fundamental organization. They must be aware that data has a source that may be slow to access or even inaccessible. As a result, they tend to be organized around a local cache instead, and a good deal of time and attention go into managing how data moves between the cache and storage.

On the right side of Figure 1.2, an alternative organization binds components to a cache that, in turn, mediates between local and cloud storage. In this architecture, components also embody the assumption that their data may or may not be in the cache. When a cache miss occurs, accessing their data will be either slow (it's retrieved over the network) or impossible (if the network is down).

Organizing around a filesystem abstraction doesn't really help resolve this problem. It's not too hard to build a filesystem abstraction that can bridge the differences between different desktop operating systems, or even between mobile and desktop operating systems. But it's the wrong abstraction for data in the cloud because it continues to assume fast, local access. These foundational assumptions can be just as easily embodied in interfaces and abstractions as code.

To be clear, how an architecture's foundational organization is embodied in its components is about much more than storage and file systems. This is one example of how an architecture lays down assumptions, and those assumptions can become wired into each line of code in each component. We'll return to this point more than once, as it's a key aspect of what makes architecture valuable—and difficult.

Their Relationships to Each Other

As programmers, we tend to place an emphasis on components over connections. The components feel material—as much as anything in software ever does—because they consist of the code we write. Components can be compiled, packaged, distributed, and delivered. They feel almost tangible.

But components aren't interesting on their own. Software comes to life when those components are connected to each other in meaningful ways. How and which connections are formed should therefore be intentional, not happenstance.

Some well-known architectures place relationships front and center. The Unix shell architecture, for example, consists of two primitives: programs and streams. Streams are directional; they have an input side and an output side. Programs read zero or more inputs and write zero or more outputs. The shell's job is to link outputs and inputs, from one program to the next, forming pipelines through which data flows.

The Unix architecture doesn't have much to say about how these programs operate. They can be written in different languages, handle binary data or textual data, and so on. Most of the programs are relatively small, focused on a single job. (The emphasis on small, narrow programs is a Unix architectural principle—more on principles in a moment.)

The relationships between the programs get more attention. By default, every program has one input stream (stdin) and two output streams. The output streams are divided into the "standard" output (stdout) and a special stream for errors (stderr). It's possible but somewhat tedious to deal with more streams, whether for input or output.

The beauty of this approach is that it's simple yet powerful. Programs written at different times by different authors can be readily combined by the user to achieve new and unexpected outcomes. And it's possible not because of constraints on the programs, but rather because of their relationships with each other.

This result, in which components are combined post-development to achieve a new result, is an example of network effects. Network effects are exciting because they produce a combinatorial explosion of value for linear inputs. And while this book isn't really about platforms and network effects, there is a deep connection between platforms, network effects, and architecture.

However, the combinatorial magic of connections can also work against an architecture. In the Unix model, programs can be combined—but they do not intrinsically depend on each other. When a system contains many interconnected components that depend on each other, these relationships become a hindrance, not a help.

When relationships are not governed, the dependency count tends to grow. And while these dependencies may be introduced one at a time, the complexity of the resulting system can grow much more quickly. It can quickly grow beyond anyone's ability to comprehend, let alone manage.

If you have ever worked on a system that had components that couldn't be touched for fear of breaking some other component, then you've worked on a system where the relationships between components have become too entangled. These scenarios demonstrate how managing relationships is just as fundamental as managing the components themselves.

Their Relationships to the Environment

Systems never operate in a vacuum. In some cases, they may be the only software running on the hardware at hand, in which case that hardware is their primary environmental concern. However, most of the time, systems run on top of or as part of some other system.

For example, consider the relationship between a program (a system) and the operating system on which it runs (also a system). Operating systems *impose* a fundamental organization on the programs they host. This organization is inescapable: The programs are started by the operating system and, to a lesser or greater extent, the operating system monitors and controls the program during execution and through termination. Without some basic agreement between the two, these programs would never run.

Operating systems vary immensely in regard to how much of the fundamental organization of a program they define. In the Unix model, for example, the imposed organization is quite limited. Programs are started by invoking a function with a well-known name ("main") and set of arguments, so those elements must exist. To be sure, the typical structure of Unix programs encompasses many conventions and APIs. But very little of that is truly required. As a result, Unix successfully and easily supports writing programs of many types, languages, and structures.

The iOS platform, by comparison, is much more opinionated. iOS applications do not have a single entry point but rather a whole set of functions they are expected to respond to. Much of this has to do with the life cycle of these applications. In the Unix model, programs start, run until they're done with the task at hand, and then exit. On iOS, applications are started, brought to the foreground, moved to the background, stopped to preserve resources, restarted due to user interactions or notifications, and so on. It's much more complicated!

On Unix, you can use the fundamental organization of an iOS program if you want to. Again, Unix doesn't impose its organization; the program designer has significant discretion. But on iOS, your application largely needs to be fundamentally organized around a model dictated by iOS. This relationship of the program to the iOS environment becomes a major driver of the program's architecture.

Relationships to Multiple Environments

More opinionated environments create tension with code reuse. Building complex applications is expensive, and many software producers would like to write a system once and use it in multiple environments. From an architect's perspective, the problem of managing the relationship to the systems' environment becomes one of managing the relationship to multiple environments.

This can be difficult to accomplish when environments impose different—and in the worst case, conflicting—fundamental organizations. There are a few standard ways in which this issue is tackled:

- Ignore the environment and organize the software in some other way. As a rule, it's expensive to develop systems this way because a good deal of time and effort go into reproducing behaviors that you could get "for free" from the environment. Furthermore, those reproductions are never perfect, and differences tend to look like defects to your users.

- Create an abstraction layer that adapts two or more environments to a single model. This strategy can work well for systems that don't need deep integration with capabilities provided by the environment. For example, it often works well with games. The abstraction layer might be part of the system, or it might be externalized. These layers are sometimes products themselves.

- Split the system into two subsystems: an "environment-specific" core that is written separately for each target, and an "environment-agnostic" edge that is shared across each. While this may sound superficially like the abstraction layer approach, it is a discrete strategy because the environment capabilities are not abstracted. In this case, the environment-specific layer becomes as deep as necessary (but, ideally, no more than that) to connect with the environment-agnostic logic.

As with engineering in general, there's no universal correct answer to the challenge of managing these environmental relationships.

Principles Governing Its Design

Until this point, the IEEE definition of architecture has focused on describing a system's current state: its fundamental organization, its components, their relationships. Now, it turns its attention to *why* it's organized this way, has these components, and includes these relationships.

Design is a decision-making activity in which each choice determines some aspect of form and function. Principles are rules or beliefs that guide decisions. Thus, architectural principles are the rules and beliefs that guide decisions about a system, helping determine its fundamental organization.

Good architectural principles assert what's important to the system—perhaps reliability, security, scalability, and so on—and guide design toward those qualities. For example, a principle might assert that a notification delivery system should favor speed over reliability. In turn, that can support a decision to use a faster but less-reliable message-passing technology.

Principles can also accelerate decision making by designating a preferred approach out of many available options. For example, a principle might state that horizontal scaling is preferred over vertical scaling. We may be tempted to think of software engineering as driven purely by facts and analysis—that is, a system either does or does not meet its requirements—but often many designs may meet the requirements. Thus, design also involves judgment calls in which we choose among a set of acceptable alternatives.

Importantly, principles govern not just what we can do, but also what we cannot do. For example, consider a system composed of a set of services. A reasonable principle for the design of this system might hold that each service should be individually deployable without downtime. On the one hand, this principle frees architects for individual services, allowing them to determine when and how they will deploy updates. On the other hand, it constrains them: Their deployment strategy must not require that other services are updated at the same time, or that those services are temporarily disabled during the update. Thus, this principle simultaneously opens up some options for consideration while closing off others.

Without constraints, teams may spend too much time exploring a potential design space, which tends to slow down decision making while producing only marginally better outcomes. It's a classic case of diminishing returns: Each new option takes significant time to explore, yet doesn't deliver meaningful benefits over options already considered. A constraint that limits this exploration will save substantial time and effort while producing just as good a result. Of course, for this approach to work, the constrained designed space must encompass suitable outcomes—so these principles do need to be carefully considered.

Too much freedom in choice also tends to result in a lack of alignment, thus undermining the system's fundamental organization. Schematically, suppose that three or four subsystems need to choose between approach A and approach B. If both approaches are roughly equivalent and no further guidance is available, the system is likely to end up with a mix of the two approaches. Because that outcome increases overall system complexity with a corresponding benefit, it's a net-negative and should be avoided. A principle that guides all of these decisions toward the same option speeds decision making and constrains the outcome, driving simplicity and alignment.

When we're not intentional about setting our principles, they tend to be set for us. And that means that we typically end up with implied principles such as "working within current organization boundaries," "minimizing scope," and "fastest time to market." None of these principles speaks to developing a better product, and they won't produce one. Establishing and adhering to principles developed through an intentional process is one of the more impactful activities an architect can undertake.

Architecture versus Design

No part of the IEEE definition better illuminates the difference between architecture and design than its assertion that *principles govern design*.

Any reasonably complex system contains hundreds or thousands of designs. These are typically arranged hierarchically: a high-level design for the system, somewhat more detailed designs for subsystems, and so on. Services, libraries, interfaces, classes, schemas—each of these requires a design.

These designs relate to each other because they describe system elements that must work together. When we consider the hierarchy of a system, we often approach design in a top-down manner for this reason. First, we'll create subsystems, defining the boundaries and their basic behaviors. Then, within each subsystem, we'll divide it further.

Each of those items (services, etc.) requires its own design, but they are not created in a vacuum. They must fit within the larger design of the subsystem. They must cooperate with their peers to realize the subsystem. Finally, they must articulate their own interior structure.

Of course, these designs don't all pop into existence, fully formed, at the same moment in time. We work in teams, so designs proceed in parallel. We expand, update, and revise so new designs are created, and existing designs are revised, over time. Unless we've mothballed a system, design is an ongoing process.

Architecture manages those designs over time. To do that, architects must think about more than just the designs. They must establish governing principles such that those myriad designs will come together into a coherent whole, both at each point in time and over the course of time.

This is not to say that architects shouldn't do design. Establishing principles for a project does no good if those principles can't be realized in the designs, and the only way this can be known is if we put them into practice. But an architect can't spend all their time on design because then they won't be practicing architecture.

And Evolution

The systems we build aren't static. Release cadences vary, but any successful system must evolve to stay relevant. This may occur through the accumulation of small changes, less-frequent major changes, or some combination of the two. But it must happen.

And so also everything we've described so far—the organization of a system, its components and their relationships, its principles and designs—must also evolve. How does that happen?

Ideally, that evolution will be governed with intention, by a set of carefully considered, fit-for-purpose principles. We can understand architectural principles as working in two ways: governing design and governing the evolution of design. One set of principles; two methods of operation.

For example, we might hold a principle that services should be loosely coupled via well-defined interfaces (a commonly adopted principle for anyone designing cloud software). This is entirely reasonable, and quite actionable when designing those services.

However, it tells us little about the evolution of those services. As we add functionality and even new services, we can maintain this property, and that acts as a sort of basic constraint on their evolution. But it doesn't address critical questions such as how to modify an existing interface, when to add functionality to existing services, or when to create a new service.

Adding new functionality to an existing system is one of the easiest forms of system evolution, and yet it can still go wrong. For example, suppose that two teams are both expanding their services with new functions. One team might choose to add a new service, favoring a larger set of smaller services. The other team might add new functions to an existing service.

When scenarios like this occur, the evolution of the system is proceeding in such a way as to undermine its fundamental organization. The problem here isn't that one approach was right and the other wrong. In the abstract, either approach could be an appropriate response to the need to expand the system's functionality. The damage arises from the differing responses, which make the system unnecessarily more complex. The principles governing the evolution of a system should head this off by articulating which approach will be used.

Adding new functionality is perhaps the easiest version of the evolutionary problem. A much harder version occurs when the principles themselves need to change. For example, perhaps an earlier principle focused on speed of delivery, so it favored designs that added code to a single, monolithic service. Later, the team might have adopted a principle of developing smaller, more loosely coupled services that can be independently updated and deployed.

Often this problem arises when teams shift from unstated design principles focused on minimizing change and quick delivery to intentional principles concerned with dependability, maintainability, and quality. When this happens, it's not enough to apply the new principles to new and updated designs. Properties such as security, scalability, and cost tend to be constrained by their weakest link—that is, the components that don't address these concerns. At the limit, to realize these kinds of principles requires every existing design to be reworked.

This is one of the hardest problems to solve in software development: how to evolve a system from one set of principles to another. At the same time, it's also one of the most common problems because the principles we care about when we're getting the first version or two out the door are often very different from what we care about once we have a successful, proven product. Our priorities quite naturally shift from shipping quickly to creating a quality, sustainable product.

One response to this challenge is a grand "re-architecture" project in which every element of the system is rebuilt to align with these new priorities. But this approach is not evolutionary—it's revolutionary. It's also rarely successful because it requires development teams to make a sustained investment in the old and the new at the same time. Add in the overhead of running both efforts, and you've easily tripled the cost of ongoing development. Few teams can sustain this kind of investment.

The good news is that an effective software architecture practice can address even this most challenging scenario. An effective software architecture team can lay out an evolutionary path for change. The key is to understand evolution not as something foisted on a system under duress, but rather as the natural state of the system. An effective architectural process makes change intrinsic, predictable, and controllable. Ultimately, the ability to govern the evolution of a system is the essence of architecture's role.

Summary

Software systems consist of components and their relationships. A system's architecture is the organization of its components and relationships, along with the principles that govern their design and evolution. An architecture describes a system in both its current and future states.

When a system's organization is not governed, decisions tend to be driven by external factors. Often these involve respecting reporting structures, minimizing the scope of change, and shipping quickly. These can be important factors, but they can work against creating a system with a clear fundamental organization.

We can better manage a system's fundamental organization by applying principles to its design and evolution. These architectural principles don't need to replace other factors—shipping quicky may still be important—but they need to be part of the conversation. Software architecture, like any engineering discipline, involves tradeoffs between competing goals.

Evolution is intrinsic to software architecture. Teams that use architectural principles to drive change over time—including adopting new principles when appropriate—can evolve their systems to deliver new capabilities and improve the security, dependability, maintainability, and other aspects of their system.

Ultimately, architecture's role in software development is to take a holistic and intentional view of the system. It begins by identifying the fundamental organization of a system, describing its components and relationships. It sets principles that govern design to realize that fundamental organization. Most of all, it's about establishing the principles via which those designs, components, and relationships will change over time.

Chapter 2
Context

Architecture is, by its nature, the antithesis of an isolated discipline. Architecture teams cannot expect to take static requirements as an input and disappear into isolation for weeks or months, only at the end producing a complete, final architecture.

Furthermore, requirements never state the complete context for an assignment. Requirements—even comprehensive ones—cannot be expected to address every aspect of a product. Architecture teams should be familiar with the product's current design, its history and evolution, its customer and market, and the channels and methods via which it is sold. These considerations all affect the architecture.

On a similar note, successful products are never truly complete. Each iteration is a step toward some later release. Those future releases may be already planned, assumed, or simply too far in the future to think about. Nonetheless, the architecture team's job is to guide a series of designs over time, and they must determine where to draw the lines for each iteration.

This chapter pulls together observations on these varied considerations. Each section offers insights that help inform the context in which architecture occurs.

Concepts

At its core, every software system realizes a set of concepts [2]. A *concept* is the logical model that the software animates but that is devoid of implementation details. For example, as a concept, mail encompasses messages, senders, recipients, and mailboxes. As a concept, mail has nothing to do with which protocol a mail application uses to communicate with a mail service (e.g., POP3 or IMAP), or whether the mail application runs in a web browser or as an installed application. In fact, as a concept, mail has nothing to do with software. Senders sent messages to recipients' mailboxes successfully, repeatedly, and for quite some time, long before the implementation that we know as email came along.

Despite their centrality, many systems fail to crisply identify the concepts they embody. That creates a space in which everyone working on that system—experience designers, product managers, engineers, architects, and so on—constructs their own view of the system's concepts. And that space tends to breed confusion, complexity, and error.

There's no such thing as a system without concepts. Concepts are how people think about systems; there's no thinking about a system without constructing a mental model of the concepts it embodies. Our goal is for everyone working on (and using) a system to have a common understanding of its concepts in number, behavior, and meaning. Without that alignment, everyone will have their own, different understanding.

That is not to say that the concepts in a system are fixed, and certainly not that they are known at the outset. Identifying and defining a sufficient and useful set of concepts is, ultimately, part of the process. Like any part of the process, concepts are best developed iteratively. They change as our conception of the system evolves, and they change as the system evolves to meet new requirements.

Still, concepts play a unique role in architecture. When we design interfaces or parcel out responsibilities to various system components, we are making architectural decisions. Architects and engineers are expected to make these decisions and, while they should be shared, they do not demand alignment with other disciplines.

Conversely, concepts must align across all product development disciplines to be effective. Concepts are realized in code, but also in the user experience, in the product documentation, and even (sometimes) in marketing materials. That does not mean that architects cannot participate in defining these concepts—they certainly should. It means that not just the architects can create those definitions; they are part of the context in which architecture works.

Concepts also distinguish one product from another. Better concepts do not always win, but sometimes they can provide an unassailable advantage. For example, consider the concept of a *user interface window*—that is, the notion that each application has its own portions of a shared screen in which to interact with a user.

Windows were not always part of computing. However, they are such a compelling concept that, once introduced, they became a dominant user interface (UI) concept. Terminals—a concept that predates windows by more than a decade—came to be subsumed by the window concept. Today, most users understand a terminal as something that appears in a window.

Of course, windows are also not precisely the same concept in, say, macOS and Windows (the operating system). Anyone who's had to switch between the two operating systems has felt the frustration that arises from working with two similar, yet not identical, concepts. That similarity without complete alignment is one reason why it's so difficult to develop software that runs elegantly on two operating systems: A much deeper adaptation is required than may be apparent at first glance.

Concepts, then, form part of the milieu in which an architecture team operates. Some exist in related systems—such as operating systems—and must be accommodated in the design. Others may be latent in the minds of your product managers and interface designers and must be extracted and understood. Finally, new concepts will arise as architecture proceeds.

Dependability

Dependability is the over-arching label for the set of related qualities that help us understand whether users can depend on a product to perform as expected. These qualities include reliability, resiliency, performance, and scalability [3].

The expected level of dependability varies between products. All products should be dependable, of course. But the minimum dependability of, say, a mobile application is typically lower than that of an identity and access management (IAM) system because a failure in the former generally affects one user and only momentarily, whereas a failure in the latter can impact thousands—or even millions—of users for hours at a time. Clearly, these extremes require different levels of care and attention.

Strictly speaking, dependability is an attribute of an implementation—not an architecture. A dependable architecture is a prerequisite for a dependable implementation, but insufficient as a guarantee. As with similar quality attributes, such as security, realizing dependability is a "weakest link" challenge: Any weakness along the way, whether in architecture, design, or implementation, will undermine the entire system. Thus, we cannot say that an architecture guarantees a certain level of dependability, but it is certainly a necessary precondition.

Nonetheless, the architecture of a system exerts substantial influence over its dependability. An architecture with explicit consideration for redundancy and fail-over, for example, will allow for more dependable designs in a way that other architectures will not. An implementation easily can be less dependable than its architecture allows, but to be more so is quite difficult.

As an interesting example, consider the problem of making a client resilient in the face of server outages. The client must detect these outages, to be sure. It must also determine when to retry its requests and when to pause requests for some period so as to avoid making the outage worse.

In a naïve client architecture, requests to services will be scattered throughout the code base. On the one hand, this seems reasonable enough: Client-side communication libraries, such as for HTTP, are typically a baseline capability of a client platform. Allowing each method to make independent requests is straightforward and the easiest thing to do, given that it requires less coordination across the teams involved.

On the other hand, this approach undermines the client's ability to have centralized knowledge of the status of a given service. Without coordination, different portions of the client might simultaneously hammer the service with requests and retries—ultimately working at odds with each other. To improve resiliency, the client needs a structure via which to keep track of all requests to the same service, track failure rates across those requests, and pause and retry in a coordinated manner. Without an architecture that addresses this concern, the client implementation has no hope of improving its dependability in this regard.

As this example illustrates, dependability generally requires accommodation at the architectural level. Without it, any implementation will struggle to meet its dependability targets. Addressing these concerns in an architecture is no guarantee of success; a design can fail to use them. An architecture team's obligation is to make them available.

Architecturally Significant Requirements

Dependability is one specific aspect of what are, more generally, architecturally significant requirements [4]. An *architecturally significant requirement* is any requirement that must be addressed in the architecture itself and cannot be left to the specifics of design or implementation. This somewhat self-referential definition can be difficult to apply in practice.

Most nonfunctional requirements fall into this category. A nonfunctional requirement is a constraint on performance and scale. Minimum throughput and maximum latencies are common examples of nonfunctional requirements. Readers may observe that the label is a misnomer: Any product that fails to meet a so-called nonfunctional requirement is, by definition, not functional; hence the use here of the more general label, "architecturally significant."

Other requirements can also be architecturally significant. A useful rubric for identifying them is to ask, for each requirement, what level of rework would be required if it were to change. Architecturally significant requirements are those for which the answer is "substantial."

Many user experience requirements are not architecturally significant. Such a requirement might specify, for example, the circumstances under which a notification is generated. If a system's architecture supports detecting these circumstances and dispatching a notification to the user, changing the set of circumstances—or even the display of the notification—is a change, but it's not an architecturally significant one.

Other data model changes can have extensive repercussions. Worrisome examples include relationships that involve "exactly one" or "never change." For example, perhaps a requirement states that a system must store an address for each user. An architecture team might be tempted to note that only one address is required, and design accordingly. That keeps the design simple—and simplicity is important—but that assumption will also become deeply embedded in the system.

In such a system, when it becomes necessary to store more than one address per user—say, one for shipping versus one for billing—a disruptive change will be required. Each use of the "exactly one" address will have to be audited to determine whether that use requires shipping versus billing. Thus, this one requirement—were it to change—would require substantial rework; hence its significance.

Noting this, an architect might instead decide to maintain a one-to-many relationship between users and addresses. Each address can be annotated with its relationship to the account: shipping, billing, or even other relationships in the future. On the one hand, this is a more complex model, albeit not drastically so. On the other hand, it is substantially more flexible. Such a model allows for significant changes to the requirements with minimal work in the implementation.

When considering addresses, we had the advantage that the requirement to store an address was explicitly given. That creates an obvious trigger to ask whether it will always be one address, and thus to prompt us to ask what would happen if it changed.

It is much harder to identify significant but unstated requirements. Here, the architecture team may need to rely on their experience in their domain to know what the requirements don't say. For example, if latency requirements aren't given, is that because they don't apply? Or are there baseline expectations from similar products—or perhaps set by the competition—that are simply going unstated?

To help uncover unstated, architecturally significant requirements, architecture teams should consider creating guidance, perhaps in the form of a checklist, for themselves and for their product managers. For each new set of requirements, run down the checklist and see what applies. Are dependency requirements covered? How about legal or compliance constraints? Have we considered which requirements might change, and how? All these questions can prompt discussion and discovery of unstated architecturally significant requirements.

Product Families

Few software products are only children. On the contrary, most have siblings. Possibly some stepsiblings, also cousins—some close, some more distant—aunts, uncles—you name it.

These relationships play out in many ways. When starting a new product, it almost always means there's no need—and sometimes no opportunity—to start from scratch. Thus, even a "brand new" product often inherits its code and its architecture, to a greater or lesser extent, from what came before it. These ties can be helpful or harmful, depending on how they're used.

To make the most of these relationships, architecture teams must be aware of and intentionally manage them. After all, these relationships are the environment in which the products are developed—and the "relationships to the environment" are part of our core definition of architecture itself.

The rest of this section presents a partial taxonomy of arrangements that can help teams identify the nature of those relationships and how to think about them.

One Product, Multiple Platforms

These days, it's common for any application to run across multiple platforms. These might be mobile platforms (iOS and Android) or desktop platforms (macOS and Windows). Targeting web browsers helps a bit but not always that much; different browsers continue to have different behavior, and mobile versus desktop behaviors still vary.

Similar considerations apply to services. Whereas some services run exclusively on a single cloud provider, many services straddle multiple providers—including combinations of private and public providers—to improve their reach, manage costs, and so on.

When running a single system across multiple platforms, architecture teams must think carefully about where to draw the line between the cross-platform and platform-specific elements. For such systems, this decision can easily be the most impactful aspect of its architecture. And, because there is no single best approach, it can often be the most contentious.

In these situations, architecture teams should work to identify the critical logic that animates a product's core concepts and arrange for it to be shared across as many platforms as possible. Generally, this logic is complex, and it's therefore advantageous to have a single, thoroughly tested implementation. This approach also results in consistent behaviors, from the user's point of view, for the core of the application.

Again, there's no single correct answer here. Many architecture teams will be constrained by existing code bases that should be leveraged, not replaced. Or, even when starting from scratch, they may need to consider the skill sets of the team they have available. Such decisions often must be taken in conjunction with their engineering counterparts.

Other aspects of these applications will undoubtedly be platform specific. The use of platform-specific technologies is typical in the user experience layer of an application, where the benefits of leveraging a platform's native UI controls tend to outweigh the cost of cross-platform solutions. Architecture teams should remember that, despite the temptation of building cross-platform UI libraries, these almost inevitably vary from native UI behaviors in ways that tend to annoy and frustrate users.

These considerations place a heavy emphasis on the boundary between the "core" portions of the application and the "edges" that vary between platforms. Defining this boundary and organizing the elements of the application around it are, of course, central to the architecture team's job.

Readers who are familiar with the model–view–controller (MVC) architecture might also note that it describes precisely the same separation between the model (core) and the view and controller (edge) that has been described here. In my experience, MVC implementations don't always achieve enough separation of the model to make this easy. Nonetheless, applied thoroughly, MVC provides a familiar approach to this problem.

Product Lines

The previous section discussed delivering a core set of functions across different delivery platforms. Sometimes, however, products are organized into a product line that offers variations on a theme. Such products are typically sold at different price points, thus keeping the simpler version less expensive—or even free—while charging more for versions with advanced functionality.

There are two basic approaches to supporting product lines. In one approach, the team produces discrete deliverables for each variation of the product. Generally, these products will mostly contain the same software. However, the higher-end, more-capable version of the product will have additional components included, thus enabling advanced functions.

Using discrete deliverables works well when it corresponds to the desired user experience. For example, perhaps you plan to sell both the "standard" and "pro" versions of your application in some application store. From the point of view of the store and the user, these are discrete (if related) applications. You may as well build and deliver two different variations. As a bonus, as the pro functionality is not included, there is no chance of a defect or hack making it available to those who haven't paid for it.

Alternatively, you can create a single deliverable with enhanced features controlled by a licensing mechanism. In this approach, users download a single application and can "upgrade" in place without downloading or installing another application. An in-application purchase experience makes this seamless for users, and it's an especially common approach on mobile platforms. The downside is that variations of the application can't coexist on the same device; there is just one version installed for the user.

These two approaches are not mutually exclusive. Ultimately, the mix of approaches may be driven by market acceptance. A business might wish to experiment over time to see whether it has more success with multiple app store entries versus a single entry with in-app purchases. The best approach might vary between different delivery platforms. In such situations, architecture teams should resist the temptation to press for the use of a specific approach and instead design for flexibility.

A basic architecture for this problem might centralize knowledge of the available functions in a single system element. The interface would make it clear that this is dynamic information; that is, it can change at runtime, as the application executes. Such an interface would include both an API for querying status and a notification mechanism through which other elements can listen for changes to licensing status.

Note that this approach is sufficient for the in-app purchase state and can also be readily used for a static decision made when an application is packaged for delivery. When functionality is packaged in or out, the interface is in some sense overkill—any functionality not compiled in will never become dynamically available. However, the other elements of the system don't need to know this, as the interface abstracts away the actual level of dynamism. Crucially, it also allows both approaches to be used within the same application for different functions.

Product Suites

Continuing our progression from close relatives to the more distantly related brings us to product suites. Whereas products in the same line tend to solve the same fundamental problem at different price points, a suite is a set of products that solve different but related problems in a familiar fashion. In offering a suite, a business hopes to compel customers to expand their purchases—that is, to buy the suite instead of individual products—thanks in part to these similarities. For customers, this approach offers to solve two related problems without learning two entirely different tools.

When architecting a product for deployment on multiple platforms, it's generally sufficient to divide a product into its core and edges, as discussed earlier. The core runs across all platforms, and generally requires some cross-platform technology to help realize this. The edge will be customized, to a greater or lesser degree, for each platform on which the product runs.

Architecting for a suite introduces a new axis for features and functions related to the suite itself. Behaviors that generally must align across a suite include the following:

- Authentication and access control. Once logged into one application in a suite, users expect to be logged into all of them (on the same device).
- Access to data. Both the connection to stored data and the experience for accessing it should, again, be shared across products in the suite.
- User experience behaviors. Users do not expect to have to learn new behaviors when moving from one application to the other; similarity is a core value of the suite.
- History and recommendations. Increasingly, applications note the actions a user has taken, making these available both explicitly (as history) and implicitly (as recommendations). These behaviors, if available, should aggregate across the suite.
- Cross-application workflows. Part of the value proposition of the suite is related solutions to related problems, so applications

in the suite typically provide a means for moving from one application to the other.

No doubt there are many other items that could appear on this list.

When discussing multi-platform products earlier, we noted the need to distinguish between cross-platform "core" functionality and platform-specific "edge" functionality. The same distinction applies to suite functionality, which lies on an orthogonal axis. Thus, a multi-platform suite architecture takes us from two parts (edge and core) to four, as illustrated in Table 2.1.

Table 2.1
Multi-platform suite architecture takes us from two parts (edge and core) to four parts.

	Core vs. Edge	
Suite vs. Product	Suite Core	Suite Edges
	Product Core	Product Edges

Even Table 2.1 oversimplifies this situation. Because the cores are singular, they need to be integrated with each other only once per product, and with their respective edges only once per platform. But the edges are per-platform, so there's a whole set of core-to-edge and edge-to-edge integrations to manage. For multi-platform product suites, this math creates a strong driver for keeping edge interfaces simple.

As this discussion suggests, architecture teams working on products within a suite must coordinate with their peers working on both the suite itself and the other products it encompasses. An architecture team must always consider the relationships of a system's components to its environment. A product suite defines just such an environment: one that is shared across the individual products within the suite.

Cross-Platform Platforms

So far, our discussion of product families has assumed that products are being developed for multiple target platforms. Some emphasis has been placed on client-side platforms, such as iOS or Windows, where user interface variation and considerations also come to the fore. Much of what has been described also applies to services targeting cloud platforms.

Architecture teams have another option when targeting multiple platforms: They can target an intermediate platform that provides consistency across different environments. Over the years, Java, AIR, Unity, Electron, and many other technologies have occupied this space, albeit with varying degrees of success.

There's no simple answer as to whether the use of an intermediate platform is an appropriate strategy for any given product. The stability and success of any system's underlying platform is a significant issue, and the guarantees—or lack thereof—that these platforms make vary widely. In adopting an intermediary, architecture teams are trading off one set of risks for another. Some of these bets will pay off; others won't.

The questions involved are a good reminder that the relationships between a system and its environment flow in both directions. It's easy to remember that a system is influenced—and especially constrained by—the environment it's operating in. Most architecture teams are aware of what the platforms they are targeting can and cannot do.

But this relationship can be made to work in the other direction by letting the system select the desired relationship with its environment. If an architecture team doesn't want to design for a handful of target platforms, then it shouldn't choose that environment. Instead, the team can adopt a cross-platform intermediary and a single environment. Conversely, if the relationship with a single environment is overly constrained, the team can elect to target multiple platforms directly. Again, the costs and risks vary, but the different approaches coexist because each is a better choice for some systems.

Finally, consider that, when selecting an environment, the choice need not be binary. For client-side devices, it's more common that it is binary; few architecture teams will try to build on top of a cross-platform intermediate for only some of their target systems.

Services, by comparison, present more of a mix-and-match environment. Indeed, some cloud providers offer common APIs for basic capabilities, albeit backed by different implementations—creating de facto cross-platform standards. Furthermore, it may be possible to pick and choose cross-platform providers for specific features (e.g., databases or machine learning libraries) without going "all in" on a cross-platform solution.

Overall, these issues concerning platform integration—the relationships between a system and its environment—can be some of the most complex parts of an architecture to address. Here, as much as anywhere, architecture teams will benefit from thorough debate, coordination, and a consistent vision.

Building Platforms

Sometimes, the products we're building *are* platforms. A platform is distinguished from other software products by virtue of appealing to two or more discrete sets of customers. For example, an operating system is sold to end users who run it on their devices, but it must also appeal to developers, who write applications that run on the operating system.

These customers are differentiated by more than just their roles. End users for an operating system include "regular" users, who use the devices to perform their day-to-day tasks, and administrators, who manage the installed applications, security settings, and the like. These are different roles, but ultimately the operating system is marketed and sold to administrators and users; they're the customers who make the decision to purchase the software.

Developers play a key, differentiated role in software platforms. As a business, a platform is a gamble on establishing an ecosystem with a positive feedback loop between users and developers that drives use, and therefore revenue, to the platform owner. Developers are essential to kick-starting this process—so much so that platform owners will sometimes pay them to target the platform.

This connection with developers means that architecture has an even more pronounced impact on platforms than it does on non-platform products. Ultimately, end users are concerned with whether the product addresses a functional need by helping them write a book, balance their budget, or manage a project schedule. And while a good architecture will help any product perform these functions well, the architecture is ultimately one step removed from the user's experience.

Developers, in contrast, interact directly with the product's architecture. In some sense, a platform is an unfinished product: It's a set of building blocks waiting to be assembled into a variety of different forms. Whether those blocks are the right shapes, whether they're easy or hard to put together—these are the outcomes of the architecture team's work to establish the components and relationships that define the system. At a certain level, a platform is its architecture.

Sometimes, it's obvious from the beginning that you're building a platform. Operating systems are, by definition, platforms. However, many products also evolve into platforms over time. For example, an application might start as a word processor. Later it might add support for macros—small programs that can tie together its building blocks in new ways. Later still it might support more complex plugins—larger programs with their own UI, storage, communication, and computation demands. This path sometimes seems unavoidable for successful applications.

An architecture team can plan for success by taking the point of view that every product is a platform—or will be eventually. With this mindset, the architecture of the system—expressed as that set of building blocks—becomes a feature, and not just implementation detail. Should the product evolve to be a platform, this investment will clearly pay off.

Even if the product doesn't evolve to support plugins or the like, this approach helps facilitate the evolution of the product itself. A good building block is a component that depends very little on its current relationships and is, conversely, ready to be connected to other components via new relationships with little trouble. The better we do at designing these properties into our system, the easier it will be to recombine and extend these building blocks to deliver new product functionality.

Standards

A standard specifies the form and function of a technology with enough abstraction to permit multiple implementations, yet with enough specificity to enable interoperability.

Standards are ubiquitous in software. They define many of the programming languages in which we write software. They define the protocols via which services communicate. They define the public-key cryptography that secures this communication. And so on.

Formal standards with wide remit tend to be produced by cooperation among multiple technology providers under the umbrella of a coordinating organization. For example, the International Organization for Standardization (ISO) exists for just this purpose. ISO and organizations like it provide the processes, framework, and infrastructure required to develop and produce its standards.

Whereas the ISO and similar organizations define formal standards-setting processes, other standards are produced in less formal ways. Many code bases, products, and organizations have "in-house" standards. These sometimes start as nothing more than how things were done at the beginning of a project; sometimes, these standards are recognized as such only when someone new tries to do things in a different way.

For example, many software companies have standards for their use of certain programming languages. These "coding standards" are especially common for languages such as C++, for which the full language is so complex that nearly everyone prefers to restrict their use to a simpler subset. The restrictions are sometimes referred to as "guidelines" or even "style guides," but they operate in the same fundamental manner as a standard.

In between formal standards and in-house practices are de facto standards—technologies with broad adoption and multiple implementations but without formal backing from a standards-setting organization. The lack of formal backing is not always an impediment to adopting a standard, and status as a de facto standard is often a stepping-stone to more formal adoption.

In some cases, use of a specific standard may be a requirement. If you're building a product that exists to provide an HTTP API to some capability, then the use of HTTP as the standard communication protocol is a given.

At other times, the context may suggest the adoption of certain standards. Perhaps your product exists to provide a service that is accessible over the network. An HTTP API might not be absolutely required. Even so, the ubiquity of HTTP in every dimension—client implementations, service implementations, developer familiarity—should be considered.

When standards do align with your architecture, you can use them to reinforce it and accelerate your work. For example, the HTTP standard assumes an architectural style that defines the behavior of clients and servers, as well as how they communicate via requests and responses. If your architecture matches this style, then adopting HTTP will help reinforce roles and expectations of client and server components, as well as communication between them. Many architects are familiar with HTTP, and they'll be able to bring that knowledge and experience to bear on your system.

Of course, the standard must work for the problem at hand. HTTP works well for some network-accessible services, but not necessarily for all of them—that's one of the reasons that alternatives exist. As a member of an architecture team, you should be happy when a standard-based, "out of the box" solution exists for a particular design problem. However, verifying the suitability of that standard is part of the job—including pushing back when a de facto standard cannot be applied to the case at hand.

Layering Standards

Because HTTP is abstract, many products use it in a particular form. That is, they codify some subset that they use, rather than allowing any use of it. For example, there are at least two different patterns for using HTTP to create resources on a server: a POST to the URL of that resource, or a POST to the URL of the container for that new resource. These are not right-versus-wrong options; they're just two different ways of doing the same thing.

When adopting a standard that provides more leeway than desired, an architecture team may want to remove such options. In the HTTP example, the team might want to use just one of these two patterns for creating resources. That will avoid the complexity of having half the system use one approach and half use the other approach.

One strategy to address this issue is to layer an in-house standard on top of a formal standard. In this case, the team can define an in-house HTTP API standard for their system. It can state, for example, that resources are always created via a POST to a parent container. That rule is entirely consistent with HTTP in general, but it's much more specific and eliminates the needless variation that might otherwise arise.

Summary

Architectural work proceeds in a milieu of considerations created by context, history, and unstated assumptions. As architects, how we choose to accommodate, react to, and leverage this environment is just as much a part of the job as designing the system itself.

Architecture teams should begin by aligning on the concepts a system realizes, the dependability that's expected of it, and other architecturally significant requirements. These considerations often go unstated if not explicitly queried, yet a system won't succeed if it fails to address them.

No product is an island, and related products create further context. The need to align with other products in the same family, line, or suite will generally constrain the design space. The platforms on which these products run—and whether they themselves are platforms—are additional critical considerations that architecture must address.

Your system's requirements, industry, and architectural style may also require or suggest technology standards that your architecture can or must adopt. An effective software architecture practice understands these many aspects of the context in which it operates and uses that knowledge to inform its work.

Chapter 3
Change

Software systems are continually subjected to forces of change. Some of these forces are direct and obvious: fixing a defect, responding to customer feedback, adding new capabilities, developing new versions. These are among the fundamental forces of change that drive software product development.

Other forces are less apparent but have an impact. Your system runs on one or more platforms, hardware and software, that are also changing. As they evolve, they may limit or remove capabilities that your system depends on, forcing your system to adapt. Or they may offer new or expanded capabilities that your system can take advantage of. There may be pressure to use these new capabilities if, say, competitive products adopt them.

Yet more changes may be induced by the larger software technology ecosystem. New platforms, technologies, and standards arise, become popular, become boring, and fall into obsolescence. These changes drive customer expectations, user expectations, and even our own ideas of which types of systems we want to build, which technologies we want to work with, and so on. There's a lot more fashion in the software industry than we would like to admit.

Absent change, we could simply design each product, ship it, and move on to our next challenge. But few, if any, software systems actually work this way. Software development today is much less about producing discrete products and much more about managing continuous changes to a running system—some of which span millions of clients and thousands of servers. Each change modifies some subset of components that must be simultaneously compatible with both current and older versions of not only other components but also themselves. Other changes occur in parallel; change is their steady state.

Change is why software development needs software architecture. It is this state of constant change that forces us to move beyond design to *design over time*. As described in Chapter 1, a system's architecture is a template for the iterative creation of designs over time. Each iteration is distinguished from what came before—but also related to it and constrained by it. Put differently, each architecture describes a set of possible designs that conform to it.

As this discussion suggests, change has become central to software development, and understanding and managing change is a hallmark of an effective software architecture practice. In this chapter, we explore and categorize change, and we delve into the factors that drive and constrain it. These discussions lay the groundwork for the process, practices, and other aspects of managing change described in the rest of the book.

Stages of Change

A useful model of change consists of three stages:

- **Motivational.** Why do we want to make this change? We might be trying to solve a specific problem, address a need, employ new technology, and so on. The motivation for a change spurs us into action.
- **Conceptual.** What do we think we will change? At the conceptual stage of a change, we choose our approach. We might replace one technology with another, optimize code or configuration, or adopt a new algorithm.
- **Detailed.** How are we going to make this change? At this stage, we work out the details involved, including, importantly, the transition from the old state to the new. That may be as simple as deploying new code or as complex as migrating data to a new database.

As illustrated in Figure 3.1, changes nominally begin with a motivation, proceed to a conceptual approach, and are then worked out in detail. As change moves forward through these stages, we're making progress.

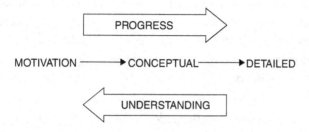

Figure 3.1
Stages of change. Each change moves through each stage, but they don't always start at the beginning and sometimes backtracking occurs.

Of course, reality is sometimes messier. It is not uncommon for discussion to start with the concept—that is, a declaration of what needs to be changed. Because it's hard to evaluate the conceptual change without understanding the motivation, such discussions might move "backward" as greater understanding is achieved.

Similar outcomes can occur during the detailed stage of a change, where greater understanding may lead to a reevaluation of the conceptual approach. Thus, while a change ultimately moves through each of these three stages, it need not be a linear progression. Indeed, a willingness to acknowledge deeper understanding and return to an earlier stage is essential to avoiding poor changes induced by the sunk-cost fallacy.

Types of Change

From the beginning, we have drawn a distinction between a system's architecture and its design. A system's architecture is its "foundational organization"; a system's design describes a point-in-time organization. A system's architecture describes evolution over time; a system's design captures a point in time. Put differently: Architecture is design over time.

Each design, in turn, describes a set of possible implementations. Thus, changes can be introduced into a system without doing architectural work—that is, without introducing a new design. Some changes can be realized within the current design.

Conversely, a change can propose a new design that no longer conforms to a system's architecture. In that case, the architecture itself needs to evolve—which alters the set of available designs. Thus, the distinction between architecture, design, and implementation is important but often blurry.

Sometimes, whether to change an architecture to accommodate a requirement is a choice to be made. Architecturally significant requirements, as discussed in Chapter 2, are precisely those that, when they come along, must be addressed by the architecture, and so force an architectural change if they are not already accommodated. It's a useful label, but we know how to apply it only after we understand the requirement's impact.

As a result of these trade-offs, we often don't know whether a change will require architectural change until we're some way into it. Our way out of this conundrum is to focus on managing change without—at least for the moment—worrying about the line between architecture and design. That is why the practices described later focus on the scope of the change, rather than its type. That is, they are written to describe managing architectural changes but apply to design changes, too. The more significant the change, the more rigor it merits, and the more closely the architecture team should hew to these practices. For smaller changes—whether to architecture or design—the level of effort can be scaled down appropriately.

Product-Driven Change

Evolving product requirements are one of two major sources of change for software systems. Products can evolve, though, in different ways and for different reasons. For a new product still striving to find market fit, the product management team might need to explore changes to its concepts, whereas the team supporting a more mature product might be focused on more minor, incremental improvements. To respond to these pressures, architects need to know more than just the next new requirement; they need to develop a trajectory for the capabilities over time.

The trajectory of a capability is an assertion about how we expect its requirements to evolve over time. As illustrated in Figure 3.2, we can think of this trajectory as being plotted against two dimensions. On one axis is the expected rate of change, ranging from zero—indicating that a capability is "done"—to arbitrarily large values for capabilities receiving significant investment. On the other axis is uncertainty, or scope of change. On this axis, a zero indicates that how the capability will evolve is well understood. As the magnitude of the vector increases along this axis, it indicates increased uncertainty about how the capability will evolve.

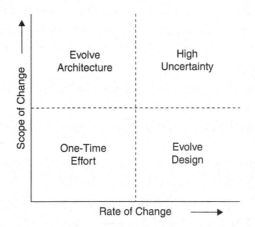

Figure 3.2

The evolution of a capability can be categorized based on its anticipated scope of change (vertical axis) and its rate of change (horizontal axis). Quadrant labels indicate how teams might respond to these forces on product evolution.

A trajectory with both a large rate of change and high uncertainty indicates a capability for which you can expect substantial new requirements, but no one is quite sure what they are yet! You'll want to tease this information out in discussions with your product management team because the trajectory vector has a direct correlation with architectural work.

Recall the distinction between a design, which is point in time, and an architecture, which is the fundamental organization of the system over time. This distinction precisely parallels the difference between requirements and trajectories. A system's current design must address its current requirements. A system's architecture, by contrast, strives to address and anticipate the trajectory of those capabilities. If you don't have a sense of which requirements are coming next, you can't really create an architecture that will support those motions.

For example, suppose that you are considering how to design a *save as PDF* capability for your application. Your product management team has given you current requirements that do not include encryption, form fields, or similar features. You've verified that those features are not anticipated for any future release, either. In other words, the trajectory for this capability lands in the "one-time effort" quadrant (lower left in Figure 3.2); it isn't going anywhere after this iteration.

Given this information, you can proceed with a simple, straightforward design. It's clear that the team's goal for this capability is to knock it out and move on. Any investment in laying the groundwork for the addition of new features in this area will be an over-investment and not the best use of the project's resources.

Conversely, suppose you learn that the trajectory for this capability is high on both axes (upper right in Figure 3.2). Now you're in the opposite situation, and you know that the current design will be only the first of many in this space. The challenge here is that, because you're in the "high uncertainty" quadrant, you know there will be new requirements—but you don't yet know what they'll be.

Here we have arrived (again) at the crux of architecture. You have in front of you not just a capability that needs a design, but a capability that needs an architecture that will support iterations of that design over time. That is, you need to not only define the components and relationships that realize the capability, but also the principles that will govern those components and relationships as the capability itself evolves. That, in a nutshell, is the central challenge of software architecture.

Technology-Driven Change

All software systems are embedded in some technological landscape, and changes in that landscape form the other major source of change. Real-time control systems might need to adapt to newer, better, and more sensors. Cloud-based systems might want to take advantage of new services that offer better performance or reduced cost. Underlying all of this, programming languages, designs, and architectural styles continue to evolve as engineers and architects evolve their ideas about how systems can and should be built.

Product-driven and technology-driven forces may align. For example, machine learning advanced what was possible from a technology perspective and, in doing so, changed user expectations about what products can do. Thus, in many systems, the adoption of machine-learning technology was driven by both new requirements and new technological options operating together.

At other times, the two forces may be opposed. For example, the development of "NoSQL" databases was a significant technological change. However, unless your product is a database, it's not likely that adopting a new database technology was a direct and useful response to product evolution. On the contrary, if your system already used a SQL database, the switching cost could be net negative, consuming development resources without producing new or better functionality.

As with product evolution, it is important for architects to understand the trajectories of these changes. Change trajectories motivated by technology, when not aligned with capability trajectories, should be evaluated soberly. It can be difficult to set aside the hype of new and exciting technology—after all, working with new and exciting technology is what draws many people into the software realm to begin with. Nonetheless, it is not too hard to enumerate the ways in which technology-driven change can lead to poor outcomes:

- New technologies may fail. They may not live up to the hype, offering no real improvement over what came before. They may even do worse.

- New technologies may offer only modest improvement. That makes them a reasonable choice for new work. For existing systems, though, our analysis must include an evaluation of switching costs. Without bigger gains, most won't pass a sober cost–benefit analysis.

Conversely, some technology-driven changes are worth investing in even when they are not aligned with product-driven change:

- New technologies may offer substantial improvements in efficiency, performance, development velocity, or other key metrics.
- Use of new technologies may be essential to recruit or maintain people interested in working on the system, especially as older technologies fall out of favor and fewer people have experience with them.

Most systems depend on many underlying technologies. It is probably unrealistic and unnecessary to identify a trajectory of change for each, let alone accommodate that much change in your work. Instead, it helps to focus on the following areas:

- Technologies that are undergoing rapid change in the industry. These are the technologies where you may want to accommodate change to take advantage of new capabilities or need to accommodate change to remain competitive.
- Technologies that are underserving your current needs, so that you will be better positioned should new options arise. For example, if your system was using a SQL database but it was a poor fit for your data model, you might have identified that as an area to monitor—and then be rewarded as NoSQL technologies arrived on the scene.

Not all technological change can be anticipated, and new technologies don't always pan out as expected. When in doubt, fall back to keeping your system as simple as possible.

Simplicity

The simpler your system, the better you can respond to any change. Architecture teams must therefore always strive for simplicity. In my experience, nothing correlates more strongly with the longevity of a system than the simplicity of its architecture, design, and implementation.

Simple does not mean weak. On the contrary, simple architectures are powerful. They achieve a lot through a minimal mechanism. They are simple yet capable because they contain a small number of powerful, general abstractions. Such systems may have many components, but those components, and the relationships that bind them, fall into just a few categories.

The opposite of simplicity is complexity. Complexity can be measured in different ways, but at its core, complexity arises when a system contains many specialized components and specialized relationships. Complex systems resist systematic descriptions because they don't have a fundamental organization. They are just a collection of components and relationships, jumbled together.

A sure sign that you are working with a complex system occurs when you find yourself thinking about specific components and relationships instead of patterns. Simple systems are governed by patterns, such as "components of type A connect via relationships of type B." In a complex system, these patterns are undermined by endless exceptions, if they exist at all.

Left unchecked, complexity will infect and overwhelm any system. Even systems that begin with a simple architecture will not maintain it without discipline. Exceptions will arise. These may be accepted for expediency or due to ignorance; it doesn't really matter. Without maintenance, entropy increases. Any system that does not strive for simplicity is already dying under its own weight.

Complexity reduces quality. When a system is nothing more than a grab bag of parts, it's easy to put those parts together in ways that don't work as expected. And it's hard to test them because the lack of structure undermines a systematic evaluation. Ultimately, the only way to know if the system works is to test the whole thing, in every variation. Few teams can afford to sustain that approach for systems of any reasonable size.

Complexity also reduces development velocity, the rate at which new work is produced. When we're changing a system, we must be able to reason—correctly, accurately, quickly—about the impact of that change. These goals can be readily achieved in a simple system governed by a small set of patterns. In a complex system, reasoning about a change requires, at the limit, evaluating its impact against every existing component and relationship. As with the quality testing burden, most teams can't sustain this cost. As a result, changes may happen slowly or not at all—and tend to break things as they happen.

Another tell-tale sign of growing complexity is justification of design changes based on *tenuous invariants*. For example, perhaps you're adding a cache to your service. You know that all changes to instances of entity A—which are stored in a different service—are currently made only by your client, so you can implement a write-through cache. The system's organization doesn't prevent other clients from updating entity A directly; *it's just not happening right now.* That's a tenuous invariant. Sooner or later, some other client will read or write instances of entity A without consulting your cache, violating that tenuous invariant, and breaking the system.

Worst of all, complexity produces more complexity. As the tenuous invariant example illustrates, once a system's fundamental organization fails, each new fix or feature introduces an essentially random change. Each new fix or feature must be evaluated, individually, against the changes that came before it. In the simplest case, it might be a new and isolated component; in the worst-case scenario, a change might introduce a whole new set of relationships that reach throughout the platform. Left unchecked, complexity always grows—it's only a question of whether it grows slowly or quickly.

Sometimes, complexity is introduced in the name of "future proofing." The general idea is to make future work less expensive by anticipating and planning for those changes now. The challenge here is that making correct predictions is difficult—especially about the future. If the prediction is wrong and the predicted change is never made, the system has taken on additional complexity with no payoff. Worse, the work done now might get in the way of the actual changes that are required in some future release. In my experience, a system is always best positioned for an unknown future by striving for simplicity, thereby making all possible future work that much easier.

To achieve and maintain simplicity requires constant attention. It requires a system with a fundamental organization based on principles that set strong constraints. And it requires evaluating every change against that fundamental organization. A change that maintains or builds on these fundamentals will preserve the simplicity of the system. A change that depends on tenuous invariants—assertions that hold now but are not fundamental—should be rejected.

Of course, none of this means the fundamental organization of the system cannot evolve. On the contrary, it must. In some sense, simplicity is maintained by insisting that changes are fundamental instead of tenuous. Such changes keep the entire system on a firm foundation.

Simplifying things is hard to do. As engineers, our instinct when faced with each new challenge or requirement is to build something new. Simplicity demands that we look for methods to solve these challenges in the context of the entire system.

Sometimes, the simpler solution may be less work. It might be that an existing component or relationship can be reused or, with a modest generalization, adapted to deliver new functionality. For example, the cache for entity A, had it been read-only with an appropriate freshness check, would not be broken by new clients. It can take more time to see and evaluate such an approach than to build a wholly new component. The advantage is that the new behaviors are added without adding complexity to the whole system.

At other times, achieving simplicity does require more effort. For example, perhaps checking cache freshness for entity A on each read is too slow. Instead, the cache needs to be kept up-to-date via events dispatched when the entities are updated. Building this notification mechanism might require substantial work. However, once it's complete, it might offer a new, general caching mechanism that can be used for all entities and clients. As a general solution, it maintains the overall simplicity of the system in a way that the one-off solution did not.

Whether that effort is worthwhile depends on the specifics of the situation, the anticipated trajectory of change, and more.

Best efforts aside, most systems gain complexity over time. Architecture teams therefore have a final responsibility with respect to simplicity—namely, to drive simplification over time. This is often best achieved by identifying latent patterns in the system. Once identified, a more general capability can be built, and the one-off implementations migrated to it and then retired. Upon completion, the system has gained a new, fundamental capability and rid itself of a handful or more of special cases. That said, if you identify something in your system that's purely superfluous and can just be removed, even better.

Achieving and maintaining simplicity requires effort. Architecture teams must constantly be on guard against creeping complexity and on the lookout for opportunities to simplify. Teams must be willing to invest, both in the short term and the long term, to maintain simplicity. Ultimately, this time and effort is all well spent.

Investment Mindset

Everyone loves a good dichotomy, and software projects are often run as if the short-term, super-tactical approach and the long-term, build-for-every-eventuality extremes are the only options for making changes. But in engineering, extremes are to be avoided and architecture teams should strive to find a pragmatic middle ground by approaching every change with an investment mindset.

The incentives for purely tactical approaches have everything to do with deadlines. In fact, that's often the only justification for quick-and-dirty changes. Has everyone agreed that the design is terrible in every regard except that it can be done more quickly than all other approaches? That's a reliable indicator that you've headed down a tactical dead end.

The problem with short-term approaches is that the only part that's "short term" is the up-front effort. Every other piece of the solution—testing it, fixing it, maintaining it, living with it—is just as long term as every other decision made on a project. Even the label is, in some sense, a lie: These approaches aren't short term; they're short-changing the project.

A short-term approach creates a myriad of long-term issues. And those issues aren't limited to, or even primarily concerned with, architecture. No one should be defending changes that damage the integrity of the product. Everyone involved should want to see a product succeed over time and should hold, if not a long-term view, at least a past-the-next-deadline perspective.

Whereas many software development roles are biased toward a short-term view, architecture has no such luxury. Architecture is not just the components of a system and how they relate; it also encompasses the evolution of those components and relationships over time. An architecture team that does not pay attention to evolution simply isn't practicing architecture.

In architecture, no change can be separated from its impact over time. Ideally, changes will improve the architecture of a system. For example, a change might simplify a system by removing an unnecessary dependency between two components. That's an unalloyed good. Whether the change addresses an urgent issue for the next release or not, the architecture team should be supportive.

In any reasonably well-structured system, most changes will occur within the existing architecture. That is, they won't make things worse (i.e., by introducing more complexity by way of more components or relationships) or better (i.e., through simplification). Rather, they'll add or evolve capabilities within the bounds and behaviors of the existing components and current relationships and aligned with the system's current principles.

These, too, are changes that architecture teams should support. In fact, any change that lies within the bounds of the current architecture should be assumed to be sound by default; the burden of objection must lie with the team. And if an objection is raised, it should be not to the specific change at hand, but rather an identification of a flaw in the current architecture that needs to be more broadly addressed.

The troublesome changes are those that hide under the "short-term" label yet degrade the system's architecture. Short-term changes to an architecture are a mythical beast; every new component and relationship is present until some subsequent change removes it.

The truth is, such changes usually aren't cleaned up later. Once a project becomes driven by short-term changes, it tends to stay that way. In fact, it tends to become more so, because the accumulation of dependencies makes it harder to get work done, which leads to more schedule pressure, which leads to more "short-term" fixes, ad nauseam. The irony of short-term fixes is that they have the long-term effect of killing projects.

Part of an architecture team's job, then, is to call out the short-term changes that aren't. And a good way to do this is to recast the short-term fix in architectural terms. It might appear that we're making a small change by adding a call from component A to component B, an architecture team might say. But prior to this change, they can observe, A never spoke to B.

What's the impact? As a rule of thumb, each new relationship will increase testing costs, because it generates new states that must be tested. It increases maintenance costs and reduces development velocity due to increased coupling. And it reduces dependability: A operated independently of B before; now it does not. Is B reliable enough to meet the established reliability guarantees of A? Perhaps it does, but at a minimum, the question must be asked, and an assessment made.

Use these questions to reframe the debate in terms of options and trade-offs, not people. Avoid framing the debate as a trade-off between architecture and engineering, architecture and product management, or architecture and anybody. When options are aligned with people and roles, decision makers are put in an awkward position: They're asked to choose winners—and therefore losers—among people who should be working as a team. It is better to assume everyone wants to do the right thing for the product and debate the options on their own merits.

Once you've identified the options, ask the team to view every proposed change from an *investment mindset*. Every change is an investment. The question to debate is whether it's a good one or a bad one. Good investments produce outsized returns; bad investments cost us over time.

We can measure returns on various dimensions. Depending on the product and the circumstances, our investments might focus on performance, operational costs, dependability, quality, or any number of other attributes. Architecture's job is to place a change in context and use that understanding to help assess the expected return along any of these dimensions. Every change persists in a system until some other change removes it.

Authority versus Accountability

It is all too common for debates that should be about the merits of one change versus another to devolve into questions of authority. I have clear memories of two different occasions early in my career when architects threw their hands up in frustration while exclaiming, "I don't know why you won't listen to me; I'm the architect!" One then literally stormed out of the conference room in which we were meeting. These were wonderful examples of how *not* to do the job!

Those individuals were confusing authority with accountability. They were confident that they knew the "correct" approach and did not want to waste time on debating options. From their point of view, their role as architect gave them authority to make those decisions and they were determined to use it. Clearly, the people working with them did not see things the same way.

Those architects should have instead focused on their *accountability*. Architects do play a unique role in software development. As an architect's job is to govern a system over time, they are well suited to assessing and understanding the impacts, both short term and long term, of any proposed change. For any given change, an architect might be the only person on the team who can see the full technical impact of a proposal.

Had these individuals taken accountability for their role, they would have approached these debates differently. They would have seen the need not to assert authority, but to contribute their insights to the debate. And if they had focused on finding a better outcome instead of "winning," they would have been open to questions and insights from others that could help everyone arrive at a better outcome.

Software development is a team effort, and everyone on the team is accountable for their part in its success. If you're eager to be an architect because of the authority you believe the role confers, you're likely to be frustrated in the end.

Incremental Delivery

Maintaining an investment mindset can be difficult if every proposed change becomes a five-year effort to "re-architect" some part of a product. Sometimes larger changes are required, but in a healthy system, these are few and far between. Most changes should be narrower, more tactical, and faster to execute. Change is best delivered incrementally.

Any big change needs to produce outsized returns to be a good investment. Problematically, the bigger the change, the more we tend to underestimate its costs and overestimate its benefits, leading to a skewed assessment.

If you've worked on a large software product, chances are you've lived through this dialog. The conversation tends to start with a small change. But as the design proceeds, the changes snowball, and the proposed investment gets bigger quickly. This part of the system is a mess, someone says, and we should just rework the whole thing while we're here.

At this point, the scope of work typically continues to expand. You started off reworking component A, but it interfaces with B. Here's your chance to redo the interface with B, which you've been wanting to revisit for some time. Of course, those changes then ripple into B, and from there into C and D. Maybe we should tackle those while we're at it?

As a thought experiment, I love these exercises. First, they illustrate the value of maintaining accurate and current descriptions of the system. If you know that changing B will impact C and D, you're in a much better place than if you don't discover that until you are halfway through the changes and the pieces won't fit back together. This is where an investment in maintaining documentation pays off; more on this later.

But these exercises are even better at generating new ideas. Some of these ideas will be good ones that could improve the system. Others will be terrible and should be abandoned. That's okay; it's better to produce a set of options and make some choices than to be stuck with no way forward. (We'll talk more about the value of developing options in Chapter 4.)

At this point, some project management teams go all in. Yes, the scope of change keeps expanding and maybe we haven't found its edges yet. But new work is exciting, these changes seem necessary, and—with a bit of wishful thinking—we can be confident everything will work out. In the meantime, nothing has been delivered; no complete changes have been delivered. Such endeavors rarely end well, and they're a hallmark of immature teams.

Other project management teams will, upon appreciating the scope of the larger changes, retrench. In the worst case, they'll resort to "short-term" fixes that bypass the current problem, but at some net cost to the product. Such changes are also poor investments: Not only do they fail to make progress on the bigger changes, but they may have made those changes harder to achieve.

Project teams can avoid this see-saw between the extremes if they can learn to balance the here-and-now with the long-term vision. As with personal goal setting, project teams can learn to differentiate between what they want in the long run and the available next steps on that journey. You might want to run a *Fortune* 500 company, but you don't start by applying for the CEO job as a college graduate.

To find this balance, architecture teams should organize their thinking into three categories:

- **A long-term vision.** This vision doesn't need to be, and probably shouldn't be, described in detail. What it should do is capture the desired fundamental organization of the system and the arguments for it, and differentiate it from the system's current state. (More on this in Chapter 4.)
- **A backlog of potential changes to get from the current state to the target state.** These are potential changes because they may or may not be made. This backlog exists to capture the ideation that occurs when considering the target state without committing to a specific plan. (More on this in Chapter 7.)
- **Current work.** These are the changes being made right now. They should be taking the project toward its vision; otherwise,

they're probably not a good investment. But they don't describe all the work required for that vision; everything can't be done in a single go, anyway.

Sometimes, the current work will grow—that's the "shouldn't we just re-architect this while we're here" argument. Assuming a vision to guide that discussion, teams can have that debate and then sort the outcome into the backlog (items to revisit later) and current work (the smaller list of items to be done now).

This might seem tricky; it requires some bookkeeping to keep categories straight. In my experience, though, it's liberating. The pressure to cram in every change right now goes away, because every change can be on the backlog for later consideration. And it avoids the temptation to discard the long-term view entirely because the current work is managed separately.

Many projects strive to make big changes over time. The best way to make that happen is to deliver a steady stream of incremental changes, guided by a consistent vision.

Architectural Evolution

Sometimes, products will be targeted to undergo radical transformations. Such changes tend to occur when driven by technology and market shifts—in other words, they are both product- and technology-driven changes. For example, the introduction of the iPhone and mobile computing spurred not only the development of entirely new products, but also triggered many efforts to transform existing products to work with and take advantage of these new devices.

Changes of this magnitude typically require correspondingly significant changes to the product's architecture. Mobile computing, for example, didn't just prompt existing products to migrate wholesale to new devices. Many of these products were reconceived as running on both desktop and mobile devices, creating an entirely new set of challenges regarding platforms, data, connectivity, and more.

As just discussed, architecture teams should strive to work incrementally toward a long-term vision and be wary of "re-architecture" efforts. But what happens when your architectural vision changes?

First, let's acknowledge that this should be a rare occurrence. If the architectural vision for a system is changing every six months, then something has gone wrong. If our target moves regularly then, even when every step aims toward that target, we'll end up taking a random walk. That will inevitably produce a chaotic, disorganized system no matter how well we manage the rest of the process.

Architecture teams should likewise be wary of changes driven by constant evolution of the technology landscape but without corresponding market impacts. The introduction of mobile computing wasn't just about technology; it also impacted users directly and created new markets. An architectural response to mobile computing was a necessity and, ultimately, delivered new value to customers.

By comparison, some technology evolutions have much more limited customer and market impacts. Microservices, NoSQL databases, and blockchain technologies may be new and exciting, but for many products, they don't translate into new customer value. If a new technology won't provide new value to your customer, it's not likely to justify the time and effort required to evolve an architecture to accommodate it.

It's tougher when the technology is relevant but late to the party. For example, a NoSQL database might be a good fit for your system, and you might certainly have chosen one if it had been available when you established your original architecture. But if you've already based your system on a SQL database and it's working well, what justification is there for changing?

Keep in mind that switching costs can be enormous. At the point at which you have one technology in production and another on the drawing board, your team has likely invested hundreds of person-years in learning your current technology. They know the theory behind it, as well as its real-world behaviors. They've learned its API, how to debug it, how to deploy it, and how to keep it running.

The latest-and-greatest alternative you're considering may indeed be better. Nonetheless, switching will require a massive investment in relearning and re-addressing every one of these concerns for a new technology. There's the guarantee that you're throwing the investment in the old technology away, and the risk that the new technology won't pan out. The bar for switching must be high because it must take all of these issues into account.

Nonetheless, for any long-lived system, sooner or later its architecture will need to evolve. That's a sign of a successful system—once that's grown beyond its original remit and is asked to do more. We should recognize that every architecture has its limits. When we reach them, we'll need an ability to adapt and evolve that architecture to keep it alive.

So, our goal here isn't to avoid evolving our architecture; it's to avoid doing it too often. And to do that, when we do revisit the architecture, we must allocate sufficient time and attention to it. A larger investment in each upgrade should lengthen the time before the next upgrade is required. A sufficient investment creates a positive feedback loop, keeping our target stable for longer.

The good news is that changes to an architecture needn't be overly difficult and, to some extent, can even be anticipated. In fact, the single most powerful technique for preparing for evolution is to have a good architecture to begin with. The better organized your system is today, the more readily and confidently you can propose, assess, and make changes. Conversely, if your current architecture is complex, poorly understood, or poorly documented, you'll need to work to address those shortcomings. Those efforts will pay off when its time for your architecture to evolve.

Some teams engage in architectural review on a regular cycle, and that can be a helpful process in managing change as well. First, it's a good prompt to stop and consider whether a system's architecture is still serving it well. Possibly the answer is yes, and no changes are required—in which case the issue can be set aside until the next review. Even better, it might highlight the need for a change before that need becomes a crisis.

A regular review can also serve as a relief valve for day-to-day work. With a review cycle in place, it's easier to maintain the discipline of sticking with current choices and avoiding unnecessary disruption. New ideas are welcome—maybe we really should be using a blockchain!—but those conversations can be deferred until the review cycle. The review cycle itself becomes the catalyst for collecting new ideas, as well as investigations and prototypes to gather more information.

Large organizations often stick to a yearly calendar that drives planning, budgeting, and so on. If you run a regular architectural review process, time it to align with the organization's processes. If your architecture needs resources to drive a big change to the system, you want to know that as planning starts. Conversely, if your architecture is in good shape for another year, then you can help the organization allocate resources to other, more pressing concerns.

Summary

Software systems exist in a constant state of change; these changes may be product driven, technology driven, or both. We can better understand change by characterizing its trajectory, and thus thinking about both its current and future impacts. As architects, how we choose to accommodate, react to, and leverage change is just as much a part of the job as designing the system itself.

Simplicity is the most fundamental method for preparing for change, so simplicity must therefore be a major architectural focus. Other things being equal, a simpler architecture will be easier to apply, maintain, and evolve.

Keeping things simple is hard work. To help keep things simple, approach design with an investment mindset: Every change is an investment in the platform; the only question is whether it's a good investment or a bad one. Strive to make good investments and to balance tactical versus strategic changes.

Finally, remember that the context in which architecture operates is itself evolving. Markets change, visions change, and technologies change. You must both start with and maintain awareness of the context in which you work. On the one hand, an architecture should not change with the latest fashions; that will generate lots of work but little benefit. On the other hand, an architecture that never changes is unlikely to keep up with evolving demands. A strong architectural practice acknowledges the need for architectural evolution and makes it a considered part of the process.

Chapter 4
Process

Architecture occurs within the context of a broader *product development process* that governs the life cycle of each product release. The software industry produces, in addition to software, an endless stream of such processes: waterfall, spiral, rapid, agile, extreme. These processes prescribe the steps—gathering use cases and requirements, designing an architecture, designing a system, designing a user interface, programming, testing, deploying, and so on—required to deliver a software product.

These processes reflect a common understanding of the need to manage change. Without change, we cannot produce anything new. Without managing that change, however, there's little chance that it will result in a shippable product. Uncoordinated change produces chaos, not software.

In this chapter, we tackle how an effective software architecture practice manages the process of change. These topics are presented independently of any specific product development process. That is possible because these topics are universal; they apply regardless of the specific methodology. An effective architecture team drives change within their organization's chosen structure and process. They may have a preferred process, but do not claim that their work depends on adopting the "right" one.

Managing change is to an architecture practice what simplicity is to architecture: the single strongest indicator of future success. When change is not managed, you have chaos. Chaotic changes tend to work against each other instead of with each other. These changes might cancel each other out, or even move the product backward by, for example, reducing dependability. Conversely, strong change management helps produce fit-for-purpose results, in a predictable amount of time, and works with any development process.

Document the System

Change never starts with a clean slate. We produce far more revisions of products than we do new ones. As a result, most architects will spend most of their time working on the next version of an existing product. Describing a system's current architecture and design is, therefore, the essential first step of any change process. If we don't know what we have now, we simply cannot make rational and informed decisions about what we will change.

If you are working on a new product, consider that even new products don't spring into existence in a vacuum. They may, in fact, be based on the code base of some older product. Or they may be intended to reuse code, libraries, or designs from prior work. Or they may be informed by experience from prior designs about what to do—or what not to do! And so on. In these scenarios, understanding the architecture of the prior systems is just as relevant as understanding the previous release of an existing product.

This may sound trivial but often involves substantial effort. Projects often place a much greater emphasis on producing working code over developing the accompanying documentation that describes how that code is structured and why that structure was chosen. Producing these documents isn't free, so unless there's an incentive to create them, it won't happen.

Such documents also require upkeep, which adds to their cost. When working on a major change—a big new feature, or a change that requires coordinating multiple teams—it's impossible to go straight from ideation to code. That creates an incentive to produce documentation to help coordinate and align everyone involved. As a result, the bigger the change, the better documented it tends to be at the start of that work.

However, as further changes accumulate—especially small ones—if the corresponding documents, diagrams, and other artifacts aren't updated, then they "rot." As the implementation drifts away from earlier thinking, documentation loses fidelity. After a few iterations, documents may be so inaccurate as to be misleading. At this point, reading one can be a hindrance rather than a help to further work, and the documentation may be abandoned entirely. Giving up on documentation, however, will just make things worse.

Working on a system without understanding its current state tends to produce failures in two different modes. The first and most obvious is that the proposed changes don't work or require far more effort than expected. Often, that doesn't become apparent until sometime during implementation, when the system starts failing. For example, the change might have assumed an invariant that doesn't hold, or what seemed like a valid input might not be. These late failures require revisiting the design, making them especially disruptive and expensive.

Needless Re-creation

More than once, I've seen a new feature be added to a product only to have the team discover later that the desired capability already existed—perhaps expressed in a different way, and certainly in some part of the system no one was familiar with. The architect might even have known that a related feature existed but, for lack of thorough investigation, did not understand how to leverage it rather than create a wholly new, yet related, capability.

While more difficult to spot, this "needless re-creation" can be even more damaging to a project than the change that fails during implementation. First, there is the obvious cost of the wasted effort. In the worst case, every single resource devoted to the duplicative feature could have been devoted to something truly new, if the team involved had only known what the product could already do. No project operates without resource constraints, making the opportunity cost of this kind of waste quite high.

This failure mode is also damaging because it breeds complexity, and complexity is software's enemy. Now the system has two ways of doing one thing where one would suffice. Two features must be maintained, yet only one is truly needed. Each subsequent change must be evaluated against both implementations, instead of just one. Customers may need to know about both features instead of just one—and they will waste their time evaluating which feature to use. These costs stick with a project and its customers forever, until and unless yet another investment is made to fold the two capabilities back into one.

If your documentation is already outdated, your teams will have to engage in a process of *architectural recovery* to reestablish their understanding of the current system. Depending on how big the gap has grown between the existing documentation (if any) and the current state of the system, this may require several different efforts. Reading the code can help, as can inspecting its behavior and data. Interviewing the people who work on the system often produces great results; many of these individuals will retain a lot of useful knowledge that needs to be captured and written down.

Should you undertake an architectural recovery effort, you will inevitably learn things about the current design of the system that you wish to change. Don't let this information go to waste! However, you should keep it separate from the exercise at hand. When recovering the current state of the system, we can't write down what we wish it was—that misses the point of the exercise. Nor can we change it as we go, because recovering the current state is the prerequisite to making those changes. Instead, these proposed changes should be captured in your architectural backlog (discussed later in this chapter).

Ultimately, an accurate view of the system is a necessary precondition for evaluating any change to the system. Without it, proposed changes cannot be accurately assessed. A proposal might be internally sound, in that it contains correct algorithms, schemas, and so forth. But if these do not align with the system being changed, then you cannot be certain that any of it will work.

Once you have an accurate and current description of your system, keep it up to date. A good way to do that is to make changes to the documentation part of your process, and the simplest way to do this is to make them an output, on par with the code itself. Just as we can verify our implementation by running tests, we can verify our documentation by reading it. Completing each change thus sets the stage for your next change, and so forth.

Work Toward a Vision

If you're conceiving of a change to your product, then you have a vision for your product that goes beyond the status quo. If you haven't yet taken the time to formalize that vision by, say, writing it down, then now is the time to do so.

An architectural vision should describe the desired architectural state of the system in a three- to five-year time frame. As noted in Chapter 3, the architecture for any successful, long-lived product will evolve in response to shifting requirements, markets, and technology. An architectural vision lays out how the architecture team plans to respond to those pressures.

A good vision is concrete without being overly specific. For example, perhaps your product does not currently support extensions, but you see a market opportunity for this capability. A vision document for this product should therefore describe adding support for extensions. It should address major considerations, such as supported extension points, and how extensions will be discovered, acquired, and installed. It should not, however, document the API for extensions; that level of detail will be added later, during the design itself.

Keeping your vision focused on a three- to five-year time frame helps set the right tone for the vision. Beyond five years, anything you write down tends to become overly speculative because, to justify thinking more than five years out, you'll need to propose a lot of work. Similarly, five years is a long time in most markets, and a vision exceeding that duration is more likely to be disrupted than realized.

In contrast, anything less than three years tends to be insufficient because it doesn't look far enough ahead. If you're always looking at just the next change, nothing serves to align the direction of travel. The real value in a vision isn't that it's right or wrong, inspired or insipid, but that it drives alignment across all the simultaneous changes to the system. If you decide you're headed in the wrong direction, you can change your vision and realign to a new target. But without a vision, changes are just as likely to pull against each other as to push in the same direction.

It's also a good idea to manage the length of your vision paper. Too short, and you won't say anything of substance. Too long, and you'll bury your reader in needless detail. I recommend aiming for about six pages of text. If you have more to say on specific topics than will fit into that page span, considering augmenting your primary vision paper with more focused papers on those topics. For example, your vision might mention integrating commerce capabilities, previously found on your website, directly into your application. A follow-on paper might focus on your vision for evolving your e-commerce systems accordingly.

An architectural vision is, along with a team's architectural principles, one of its essential outputs. Developing your first vision document requires significant effort. Plan for time to gather input from your stakeholders and research relevant technology and market trends. Set aside time for the team to generate multiple options and engage in debate. Give your stakeholders—including engineering and product management—an opportunity to review drafts and incorporate their feedback. When you're done, publish your document as widely as practical.

Once you've published your vision, plan to revisit it regularly. Unlike revising your system documentation and creating an architecture, updating a vision paper is not something that's done with each change. Assuming a three- to five-year time frame, an annual refresh works well. During that year, you'll have made significant progress toward achieving that vision; you may be able to remove some of what's accomplished, and you have the opportunity to extend your thinking by another year.

Many times, even the annual update may be modest. That's a good thing: Again, the point of the vision is to align work in a common direction of travel. That shouldn't be changing too frequently. Periodically, however, you may see bigger changes due to market or technological disruptions. A significant revision to the vision document helps signal to everyone involved that such a change has occurred.

Write Change Proposals

Just as it's valuable to write down the current and envisioned future state of the system, the changes we propose to take us from current state to future state should likewise be written down as a *change proposal*.

A complete change proposal addresses all three stages of a change: its motivation, its conceptual approach, and its detailed design. But the point of the change proposal isn't to start by sorting all that information out. Rather, change proposals provide a container in which we can gather this information as the proposal develops.

A change proposal can begin with nothing more than a sentence or two describing why a change is needed (its motivation) or what might be changed (its concept). A good early revision of a change proposal focuses on big-picture questions such as whether the change will address new requirements, and how it aligns with our vision for the system.

Early-stage change proposals can also describe what is to be changed, such as which system components or relationships will be evolved. But they need not—and probably should not—describe precisely how that change will be realized. It's better to get alignment on the motivation and conceptual approach first.

Change proposals are the core mechanism by which you capture, debate, and refine the proposed modification, so they need not be polished to begin with. If you have a specific change in mind, then the change proposal can, of course, make that clear. For example, maybe you are proposing to adopt a new architectural principle for your system; that's already quite a specific modification. But the point here is to capture every proposed change, whether it might be architectural or not. Early on, the scope of change need not be known. Perhaps your proposal for a new principle will evolve into, say, a modification of some existing principle.

Some change proposals will, over time, move on to detailed designs. A design is a specific and detailed description of how something—a feature, an algorithm, a service—will work. A change proposal that makes it past conceptual approval will move on to the design phase. The design process is covered in more detail in Chapter 5.

For example, suppose you have been asked to address a new requirement that your system, which stores textual records, should support text-based searches of those records. A corresponding change proposal might be to enable and leverage the built-in text search capabilities of the database storing those records. After you approve that conceptual change, you'll still need to work out the detailed design for that change. At the concept stage, a change proposal simply narrows things down to which components will be revised.

Not all change proposals will require a detailed design. For example, a change proposal might suggest an addition to your vision. A vision is neither your system's architecture nor its design, but rather a statement about future direction. Updates to your vision are changes: They require updating the vision document, and they should be managed via your change process. But they don't require design work per se.

We tend to think of changes as being additive because product development places a heavy emphasis on building out new features. However, we should not automatically equate making a change with making an addition. Changes can also remove features, modify existing features (perhaps to make them faster, cheaper, or more scalable), or modify other aspects of the system.

Meta-Changes

While levels of formality vary between teams, some teams make a point of rigorously documenting their change process—that is, the practices they use to manage changes. But how do you change the change process? With a change proposal, of course.

These "meta-changes" might seem over the top to some, but others find something satisfying about creating a process capable of updating itself. Regardless, my experience is that teams find the uniform application of a change process democratizing: Anyone can propose any change, and each change will be given a fair shake. That doesn't mean all changes are accepted, of course—far from it.

Maintain a Backlog

As described in Chapter 3, each change to a system goes through three logical stages: identifying its motivation, developing a conceptual approach, and working out the detailed design. Although the flow through these stages is not always linear, your process should nonetheless explicitly track each change through each stage. Such tracking ensures that, even if you start in the middle, you don't proceed with a conceptual approach without agreeing on the motivation or develop a detailed design before you're aligned on the approach.

The list of current, past, and future change proposals, along with their current stage, forms your architectural backlog. The notion of maintaining a backlog is strongly associated with agile software development practices, although the basic notion of iterative and incremental development, and thus the need to keep track of what might be done next, precedes agile by decades [5]. The alignment here with the agile nomenclature is deliberate; assuming your organization uses agile practices in some form, then the notion of maintaining a backlog will be broadly familiar and easy to explain.

But do not confuse the architectural backlog with the product backlog. The former should contain change proposals, describing architectural work; the latter will describe features, capabilities, or functionality. The two are related, but do not have a one-to-one correspondence. For example, some items in the product backlog might correspond to multiple change proposals, either because alternatives need to be evaluated or because several changes are involved. Conversely, other items in the product backlog might have no corresponding change proposal; not every new product feature requires architectural work.

As mentioned in the previous section, documentation during the motivation and concept stages of a change can be brief, on the order of a few paragraphs. Thus, at these stages, the backlog entry for a change proposal can serve as its documentation. However, during the detailed design stage, you'll need more expansive documentation. Chapter 5 is devoted to the design stage, and Chapter 7 provides additional guidance on managing your architectural backlog.

Consider Alternatives

If the conceptual phase generates only a single approach, then moving on to designing that change might occur fluidly. The lack of alternatives eliminates the need for debate, and even making a formal decision to proceed may not be needed. This outcome can be both reasonable and even common for development processes that work in smaller iterations, and thus demand smaller, more incremental updates to a system's architecture. When making smaller changes, it's simply more likely that adherence to the current architecture will point to a single way forward.

Nonetheless, the conceptual stage provides the best opportunity to generate and compare alternatives. Continuing the earlier example, an alternative proposal might suggest meeting the same search requirement by adding a separate search engine to the system, rather than using the intrinsic database search capabilities. The motivation is the same, but the conceptual approach differs. Both concepts will meet the requirement, albeit with different costs and different performance characteristics. Creating space for multiple proposals helps spur divergent thinking, and thus the development of alternative concepts.

Figure 4.1 illustrates how a set of proposals might relate: Multiple concepts provide alternative approaches to a single motivation, and multiple designs for a single concept. Most of these will be rejected, but that should be understood as a healthy part of the change process, rather than a failure.

Early exploration of alternatives can also produce better results from a planning and execution standpoint by increasing predictability. To see why, consider what happens if architects proceed with their first idea instead. At first, they seem to be making great progress as the change is worked through in increasing detail. Then, generally late in the game, issues may arise. Every change has its downsides, so this always happens; it's only a matter of whether such issues are identified early or late. When issues are found late, the design may need expensive corrections. In some cases, an entirely different conceptual approach might be required.

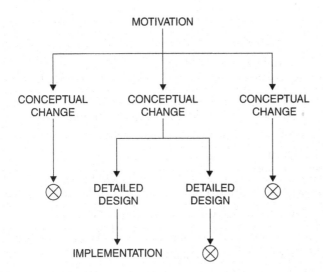

Figure 4.1
For nontrivial changes, one can explore multiple concepts that speak to the same motivation. Similarly, different detailed designs can be created for the same conceptual approach. Typically, at most one proposal will make it through the process and be implemented.

When issues are identified late, even the question of whether to explore alternative conceptual approaches becomes fraught with stressors. Some participants will, quite naturally, be more attached to the current approach thanks to our cognitive biases in favor of what we've already invested in. It's also difficult to create an informed comparison with potential alternatives. Those alternatives aren't well developed yet, so they may look great in comparison—in the same way that the now-problematic approach looked great when it was first started. In such situations, a good deal of time and energy can end up being redirected from working on the change to just deciding how to proceed. In the meantime, the clock is ticking.

When there are alternatives to consider, they should not be embedded in a single proposal. Continuing the example, a proposal that adds text-based search capabilities by either using the existing database or adding a separate search engine isn't helpful; that's just a restatement of the motivation in a different form.

Forcing each alternative to be treated as a discrete change proposal, subject to review and evaluation, helps structure the debate. Maintaining each proposal as a separate item in your architectural backlog also provides a clean record of alternatives that were considered and rejected. Instead of a single proposal with a long and convoluted history, you'll have a short list of proposals with an explanation of what happened to each.

This last point emphasizes that proposing a change is not a pro forma process. Clearly, some proposals will make it past the conceptual approach stage—otherwise no progress is made—but some, perhaps many, will be rejected. Nor does rejection mean that the proposal was flawed; it might simply have lost out to an alternative that was better by some relevant metric.

A strong architectural practice develops many conceptual proposals and rejects a substantial portion of them. When this is achieved, it indicates that two critical behaviors are happening.

First, it signals that the team is creative and capable of producing a variety of approaches for consideration. The first idea that occurs is not necessarily the best one, but even if it is, that can hardly be judged in isolation. Developing a set of alternatives tends to produce more thorough understanding and, ultimately, better outcomes.

Second, it encourages broad-based contributions. Some architects are prolific and can produce a variety of approaches on their own, but we all have our preferred approaches and biases. By encouraging the development of more alternatives and normalizing rejection, a team creates the space for other points of view and ideas to emerge and be shared. Those specific proposals may or may not be selected, and it's important to avoid turning the process of winnowing them out into a competition. Even the process of assessing rejected proposals can help strengthen the one that is approved.

Should a major change be considered without divergent approaches naturally arising, take steps to spur the creation of some alternatives. If asking the team for alternatives isn't working, try making some suggestions yourself. They don't need to be good ones, and it might even be better if they aren't. I have been known to suggest alternative approaches that I would never accept because I thought it would prompt others to respond with better ideas, and I've rarely been disappointed. At this stage, the proposed approaches are also likely to be variations of each other, combinations of other approaches, and so on.

Staying organized helps as well. In your backlog, link related proposals to each other and to the requirements they address. When deciding on a concept approach, decision makers should have this information readily available.

Of course, generating too many options creates its own burden. As a rule of thumb, I'd consider more than four or so related conceptual approaches to be more than necessary—even for a major change. At the same time, keeping the level of effort required for each conceptual proposal relatively lightweight keeps this part of the process from becoming unnecessarily burdensome.

If you have two or more competing proposals, sooner or later you'll need to select one alternative. If you can't immediately make this decision based on the change proposals alone, you can decide to proceed with detailed design for more than one approach, knowing that later you'll select only one of them to implement. However, you should try to minimize the number of proposals carried forward to the detail design stage because investing in each one takes effort, and that effort should be well spent. Don't let moving forward with multiple proposals be a crutch for poor decision making. (Decision making is covered in detail in Chapter 5.)

When choosing among alternatives, you also have an opportunity to assess whether a single change proposal can address a broader set of needs. Sometimes this may be obvious, such as when several related requirements clearly call for a common solution. However, bigger gains are possible when architects can identify disparate requirements that can be addressed with the same underlying mechanism. When evaluating change proposals, the broader set of architectural considerations, your vision, and related requirements can all bolster your analysis.

Finally, it's important not to linger too long at the conceptual stage. If a proposed change is straightforward and there are no alternatives, it should move ahead quickly. And while more time is required when there are complex alternatives to evaluate, no decision should be allowed to drag on unreasonably.

Not Doing Things

Being in the business of developing and shipping software, there's a reasonable tendency to assume that a successful change is one that proceeds to implementation, ships in some future release, and is ultimately used by customers. That is often—but not always—the case.

A strong change process tends to force clarity on many points, including

- **The problem to be solved.** The initial work might have been based on requirements that were unclear, were incomplete, or misrepresented the desired functionality.
- **Implementation cost.** Each change is an investment, and not all investments offer a good return. The process of developing a proposal may make it clear that its cost will exceed any reasonable return.
- **Operational cost.** Cloud-based services incur ongoing operational costs for compute and storage resources. Changes for embedded systems may impact hardware component costs by, for example, requiring a faster CPU.

For these and other reasons, the outcome of evaluating a proposal, or set of related proposals, may be a decision to reject all of them.

A rejected proposal is not a failure. On the contrary, it is far better for an organization to identify such issues during the conceptual stage than during detailed design, implementation, or after release. The sooner such a decision is made, the more waste is avoided. To help an organization avoid going down expensive, dead-end paths is one of the most valuable things an architecture team can do. A strong change process is not just about how to do things, but also about what not to do.

Urgent versus Important

An architectural design process will not be especially effective if blindly applied. Its application should take circumstances into consideration.

When work is urgent—truly urgent—it is unreasonable to suggest that complete system documentation must be developed, and vision papers updated, before the design process can proceed. Security, legal concerns, and other exigent issues may dictate circumstances and deadlines that can be neither ignored nor negotiated away. When urgent work arises, teams must do their best based on what they have at hand.

Indeed, the only good time to prepare for urgent work is before it arises. Some teams consider recovering and maintaining architectural documentation to be a tax, but it's more like an insurance payment. It has a cost and there's some uncertainty as to when it will be needed, but sooner or later disaster will strike. Rigorous system documentation is one of the best investments you can make to prepare for an emergency.

If you find it difficult to find time for a disciplined change process—the kind that produces and maintains accurate system documentation—it may help to recognize that most of your work is important but little of it is urgent. Shipping a new feature on some arbitrary deadline is important, but it's not urgent. Short-circuiting your process for work that is not urgent undermines preparedness. It is your important, not-urgent work that most deserves to be tackled carefully and thoroughly.

Does your team have work that isn't important or urgent? Don't do it—spend your time on getting the important stuff right.

Redocument the System

The final step in managing change brings us back to the beginning: We must document the system in its new, changed form. Only then have we closed the loop and prepared ourselves to tackle the next change.

The effort involved here will, of course, depend on the scope of the change. As you worked your way through the change proposal, perhaps you narrowed its scope. Perhaps no architectural changes were required. The required updates might be limited to modest changes to a single document.

Of course, changes with a broader scope of impact will require more work. Although change proposals should not be allowed to grow too large, even a targeted change might require broader updates. For example, the addition or revision of an architectural principle might require changes not only to the documentation of those principles, but also to standards, architectural documentation, and even design documentation that reference that principle.

When updating documentation, you may identify additional changes that should be made, or at least considered, because of the current change. Those should be captured as new change proposals and added to your backlog.

Finally, interested parties should be made aware of these updates. Communication is covered in more detail in Chapter 8.

Change Proposals as Pull Requests

Current software development practices use pull requests in a manner broadly like the change process described here:

- Start with a baseline description of the system, as coded.
- Create a proposed change that can be viewed as a "diff"—that is, as the differences from the baseline.
- Share the proposed change as a "pull request," using that to collect feedback and share further refinements.
- If approved, "merge" the pull request, thereby updating the code.

The process of "merging" a change proposal into the current system documentation is still far more manual than applying code changes by merging a pull request. Perhaps that will change in the future. In the meantime, the analogy can still serve to help explain the change proposal process.

Summary

Change lies at the core of software development. Change should not, however, be an unstructured or undisciplined activity. Effective software architecture practices use a change process through which the architecture team can explore alternatives, minimize backtracking and duplication, and stay focused on their most important work.

Figure 4.2 illustrates the architectural change process. It begins with a description of the system in its current state, which must be recovered from the implementation if not already available. And it requires a vision of what the system can be at some time in the future, informed by the context in which the system is developed and operating.

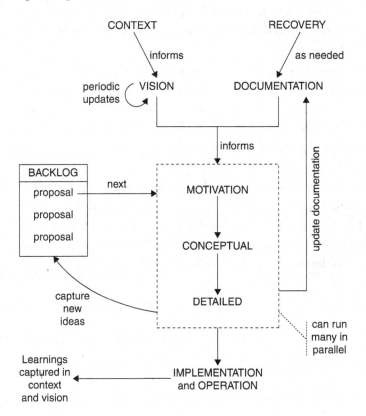

Figure 4.2
Summary of the change process. Context, vision, recovery, and documentation activities and artifacts inform the three stages at the core of the process. The backlog keeps track of current, potential, and past changes.

The core of the process focuses on change proposals, which capture changes as they move from motivation, to concept, to detail. Teams should use an architecture backlog to track past, present, and future change proposals. When a change proposal is first selected from the backlog, it is typically at the motivation or concept stage. It is possible, however, that a more complete proposal was returned to the backlog and has now been picked up again for further work.

As proposals are developed, alternatives may be suggested, and new proposals with different motivations, concepts, or detailed designs may be generated and evaluated. Some of these may be further developed in parallel—although at any time, proposals can be moved to the backlog for later consideration.

When a change proposal is approved for implementation, the system documentation must be updated to reflect the new, changed state of the system; this up-to-date documentation will serve as an accurate baseline for future work.

Throughout the change process, teams should keep in mind that not all changes will be completed. Some will be abandoned as not worthwhile; others may be abandoned because they don't work out. A strong change process identifies these situations as early as possible, rather than focusing on delivering every change.

Finally, architects should stay engaged with these change proposals as implementation work proceeds and the changes are deployed. Lessons learned at these stages are too late to be reflected in the now-approved change proposal, but they can and should impact future work. That might take the form of new change proposals or otherwise be reflected in the context and vision that guide the process of change.

Chapter 5
Design

At this point in the process, we have an accurate and comprehensive description of our system, we're aligned with a guiding vision, we've proposed a few changes at a conceptual level, and selected one to move forward with. Now—finally—it is time to move on to detailed design. Note that here we use the term "design" to apply equally to design of architecture—sometimes called "architecting"—as well as design of the system according to the current architecture. Whether you're doing one, the other, or both depends on the change being made, but the activity of design doesn't differ.

Design is an intellectual problem-solving activity. It takes a statement of the problem as its input—in software development, these are requirements—and produces a specification of a program that, when implemented, will solve that problem. Making the leap from the problem to the solution can feel a bit like magic.

Indeed, some architects practice design as black art. They'll disappear for days or weeks with a design challenge in hand and return with a wholly formed solution. I have no doubt this works for a few talented individuals, but I don't recommend it. An open, structured approach to design tends to produce better outcomes and—crucially—helps teach design skills, thus creating effective and resilient teams rather than a reliance on a singular ability.

Humans are intrinsic problem solvers. Faced with a problem, we're willing to experiment with new ideas and try new things. Some of these will work! And armed with our memory of what's worked before, we often have a solution—or at least the start of one—for the next problem. If most software products were simple, this might be enough for software design, too.

The products we're addressing here, though, tend to be massively complex. They may consist of hundreds of discrete elements and millions of lines of codes, and have hundreds or thousands of people working on them. Also, they're often trying to solve some new problems, because it's the nature of product development to strive for something new and differentiated. These are not problems for which we'll find an immediate solution by referring back to those we've tried before.

When managing a design process, it helps to recognize that we can structure the design process as three steps: decomposing larger problems into smaller ones, addressing those smaller challenges, and then composing those solutions to solve the larger challenge. Providing this structure is essential to managing architectural design.

How Architecture Accelerates Design

Design is a creative activity. To design something is to will into existence something new. It requires skill and knowledge, but also imagination and persistence. In the beginning, anything is possible.

This endless expanse of options is, of course, terrifying. The job is to produce a design—just one—to address some need or set of requirements. Working through an infinite number of options is a lot of work—certainly more than can be completed under a deadline.

Clearly, no engineer considers an endless set of options. In engineering disciplines, the set of design options tends to be constrained to a menu of options. For example, consider a civil engineer who needs to bridge a chasm. They do not generally begin by inventing new types of bridges. On the contrary, there's a basic set of types from which they'll choose: beam, truss, cantilever, arch, and so on.

This fixed menu does not make the problem of designing a bridge easy. Different types of bridges have different properties, including their span, rigidity, materials, method of construction, and so on. Civil engineers would have an easier job if a single type of bridge was superior in all respects, but life is not so simple. On the contrary, multiple types of bridges exist because the demands placed on bridges vary so widely.

When selecting a design for a bridge, a civil engineer will be constrained by external factors. For example, the distance across the chasm and its depth might allow some designs and prohibit others. The engineer might wish to use other options, but the chasm can't be changed; the design must accommodate it.

Thus, to design a bridge is to will into existence something entirely new—a bridge that has never been built before and will never be built again—and yet to do so within the constraints of the available options. This "creativity within confines" is the fundamental engineering challenge—whether for bridges or for software.

In software, we often suffer from fewer constraints. Software systems tend to be so flexible and so malleable that it often feels as if any approach can be adopted. To some extent, this is true. Software engineers rarely encounter rigid, external constraints of the type that bridge-builders must face down.

Software engineers tend to react to this flexibility in two ways. The first reaction is to fall back on what they know. For example, imagine they are building a service that must concurrently handle many API requests. An engineer familiar with event-driven programming might adopt that design because it meets the requirement and it is, after all, familiar to them. There's no need to learn a different approach, which would require more work and make it more difficult to meet the deadline.

The other typical reaction is just the opposite—to try something new. Another engineer familiar with event-driven programming might believe that approach is old news, having heard that multi-threading is the way to go. Adopting a new design has some associated risks, but also potential upsides. The design might indeed work better. Moreover, learning something new keeps engineers engaged and broadens the skillset of the team. The next time a similar solution is needed, the team will have experience with both event-driven and multi-threaded approaches.

Unfortunately, while this flexibility might seem to be an asset, in practice it can undermine the integrity of large systems. Problems arise when these design choices are made locally and in an isolated fashion. Without governance, it's all too easy to end up with a system that uses an event-driven implementation for one API and a multi-threaded implementation for another.

In isolation, both approaches might work. In combination, the complexity of the system has just been substantially increased without any commensurate gain. The ability to share code between the two APIs has been limited, if not eliminated entirely. Developers will find it harder to work on both APIs because they must switch between two very different sets of rules. It will take twice as long for defects to be worked out of the system because the two approaches tend to have different failure modes. They also scale differently, so improving performance will be twice as hard as it otherwise would be.

Almost paradoxically, too much flexibility creates a drain on the system. During design, it increases the number of choices to be made; during implementation, it increases the amount of work to be done.

These situations are where architecture as constraint comes to the fore. In software, we don't have the luxury of an unchangeable chasm and available building materials dictating our approach. Therefore, to maintain the integrity of our systems, we must impose our own constraints. Those constraints—as articulated by the principles that govern the design of the system—are the system's architecture.

A good architecture accelerates design by imposing constraints that prune options. Need to handle concurrent API requests? An architecture that imposes a specific approach eliminates the time spent choosing between options. It creates the opportunity to share code throughout the implementation. And it creates opportunities to leverage people, testing, and scaling work across a single, uniform design.

How Design Forces Architectural Evolution

None of this means that every design must be completed from a menu of preexisting options. If it did, we'd all still be crossing beam bridges made from unhewn logs—when we crossed a bridge at all. Sometimes the available options don't meet the requirements and a new approach is necessary.

Although much of an architecture team's job is to lay out constraints on how known, well-understood problems can be solved, the flip side of this responsibility is identifying when existing solutions aren't good enough and something new is required. Developing new solutions and incorporating them into the project's architecture is critical work and needs to be treated as such. These issues should be identified as early as possible and receive sufficient attention.

Sometimes we are tempted to address novel problems as part of our regular workstreams, but this is a risky approach. The need to solve a new problem is best handled by acknowledging the uncertainty inherent in this process. Prototyping and research are appropriate, and dedicated people and time should be set aside in the schedule to explore options. This requires patience and investment up front but will be rewarded when the result of that work is adopted consistently and successfully throughout the project.

At other times our options change—such as when steel became available for building bridges—and we should remain aware of new and better approaches that we might wish to adopt. Here, again, architecture teams must guard against the willy-nilly adoption of or experimentation with new techniques throughout a system because such work will undermine the system's integrity.

The point here is not that you should suppress all experimentation, however. Some amount of experimentation should be conducted because it can lead to new and better ways of doing things. It can also be a key ingredient to keeping some of your best talent engaged and interested. Rather, the point is that you should manage the experimentation.

Create a space for experimentation by pulling it out of the normal product development cycle. First, this approach helps clarify the investment in new ideas versus straight-line production costs; that clarity will aid everyone involved. Second, it can allow for greater experimentation because this work won't be on the hook for meeting a critical deadline. Finally, it allows experiments to fail without disrupting plans for shipping. This last point is critical because, if you're doing your experiments correctly, some of them will fail! Making production work dependent on an experiment puts your product delivery at risk and undermines the experiments by removing the team's option to acknowledge failure when it occurs.

Returning for a moment to handling concurrency in API requests, it turns out that neither the event-driven approach nor the multi-threaded approach is, on its own, superior. A hybrid approach can outperform both: An event-driven approach maximizes what each thread can accomplish, but multi-threading is necessary to scale beyond what a single thread can accomplish.

Thus, a system aiming for a scalable concurrent architecture can reasonably use both approaches in combination. In other words, a possible architectural constraint on such a system is that the API implementation must be implemented according to hybrid event-driven and multi-threaded models—rather than one or the other.

That's a complex outcome, and one that's unlikely to be the correct choice in every case. Any given system might not have the scaling requirements that justify the additional complexity. Or, they may be constrained by the choice of programming language, framework, or some other factor, which supports only one approach or the other. Nonetheless, it's a compelling example of the choices an architecture team must make, of the need for teams to be aware of the choices available to them, and of the kind of design questions for which an architecture ought to provide an answer.

Decomposition

Unless you're tackling a simple design challenge—and that does happen, of course—the first step in design is decomposition. Faced with a large and complex problem, we divide it. If we do this well, then each of those parts will still require further work but solve a smaller and more manageable problem. And we can do this recursively, until we've reached a set of problems that we know how to solve.

In fact, we've been applying decomposition from the beginning of this book, albeit without labeling it as such. To describe the architecture of even a modest system is a big, complex problem, so we immediately broke that down into pieces by describing a system as a set of components and relationships operating in some environment. Components, relationships, environment—that's decomposition in software architecture.

We applied the same move when we broke the change process down into phases: document the current system, align with a vision, develop change proposals, design a specific change. It would be very hard to do all these things at once, so we break them down into separate phases. Each has its challenges. Even describing the current state of the system presents challenges in capturing and describing a lot of information. Decomposition is, again, our basic technique for dealing with complexity.

Applying decomposition during the design process, then, isn't adding a new technique to our skills repertoire. However, we sometimes face an added challenge at this stage. When we consider the architecture of an existing system, its decomposition into components, relationships, and environment is predetermined. However, when we are designing a new system, or making significant changes to an existing architecture, we have the added challenge of selecting an appropriate decomposition. At this stage, architects cannot rely on a decomposition being handed to them. Instead, they must be aware of what makes for a good decomposition, and they must be able to propose and evaluate some possible decompositions against those criteria.

Generally, decompositions should strive for simplicity. Remember, we're applying decomposition to a problem because it's already too hard to solve in a single go. Our goal is to break the problem down into more manageable pieces. But if we can't keep track of those pieces, what they do, or how they relate, then we haven't improved the situation—and we may have made it even worse.

A good decomposition keeps things simple first by introducing a manageable number of elements. If this number is too small, then the decomposition hasn't gained us anything; we'll find ourselves breaking down those same elements again to design them. However, if we have too many elements, we've created a new problem—managing the relationships among them.

A good decomposition also defines elements that abstract away details. Again, this speaks to the core of why decomposition works: It divides one problem into many subproblems, each of which is smaller and can be solved independently. If the decomposition doesn't carve off enough into each element, then it doesn't help us achieve this goal. We want to break the problem down into elements that isolate these problems.

Software design is an interesting pursuit because there's no simple answer to these challenges. We can't say, for example, that every decomposition should break a problem down into six smaller pieces. Six isn't a bad target—it's enough to create some division, but not so many as to be overwhelming—but it's impossible to say in the abstract if it's suitable for any given problem.

Composition

Decomposition isn't enough to build a working system. We can break a problem down into pieces and solve every one of them, but if we don't put the pieces back together, we don't have a working system. We must compose the pieces back into a cohesive whole to realize our design.

In some sense, this is a trivial observation. At any stage of the process, a decomposition that can't be stitched back together to solve the larger problem isn't functional. Thus, as we decompose a problem, we are anticipating how the pieces will come back together to form a solution. At this basic level, decomposition and composition are two sides of the same coin.

Nonetheless, composition presents its own challenges and opportunities. Here, simplicity and efficiency are paramount. If we break a problem down in such a way that putting the pieces back together is a convoluted endeavor, then we're creating a complex solution. That will make composition hard to do, hard to get right, and hard to maintain. The relationships between the individual elements should be as straightforward as possible.

A poor breakdown might also lead to inefficient interactions. For example, relationships between logic components (which execute some process) and data components (which store records or content) often focus on one item at a time. That keeps the simple case simple but doesn't work well when the logic must operate at scale on many records. To work efficiently at scale, the relationship between the two components shouldn't be record-by-record, or at least not only so. Instead, it should describe relationships based on batches or streams of records, thus permitting an efficient composition.

As this example suggests, composition depends heavily on the interfaces to the individual elements. Are you breaking a problem down into two pieces to be addressed by separate services? If so, you're also creating a cross-process, and possibly cross-machine, boundary between the two. Will that (relatively) high-latency interaction suffice, or will it be too slow? If it's too slow, a decomposition into libraries or classes within the same service might be necessary—and might reduce the latency between the components by many orders of magnitude.

Composition is also aided by standardization. When a system consists of many components, a lot of time and effort can be spent wiring those elements together—whether that happens via function calls, network requests, or message-passing. If the system uses a heterogenous set of mechanisms, a good deal more time and energy will be spent translating from one mechanism to another. A system that standardizes a minimally sufficient set of mechanisms will, by applying this constraint to the design of each component, reduce or eliminate these impedance mismatches.

Composition and Platforms

When we're designing a specific capability, we can plan a decomposition and composition that address the problem at hand. If we do this well, we also lay the groundwork for new compositions, ones that the design didn't plan for or anticipate.

This observation is, of course, the intuition behind code libraries and other forms of reuse. When we break a problem down into discrete elements, we can readily ask what other uses we might have for them. A modest broadening or generalization of the interface might significantly expand its applicability.

During the design process, we can also look for recurrences of the same problem. Perhaps two different parts of the system both require an element that requires text processing. They may not need precisely the same set of functions, but they'll likely have a lot of overlap—especially if the rigors of multilingual support are considered. This creates an opportunity to create a single, shared element that can be integrated back into the discrete parts of the system.

For the most part, these discussions assume we're building an application, or perhaps a family of applications. One way to think about an application is as a precomposed set of components, organized to provide the set of capabilities that constitute the application itself. From this point of view, the difference between an application and a platform is that a platform leaves the assembly to the user—or the developer. That is, a platform is designed via decomposition, but with the intention of producing a set of components that can be combined in ways not originally anticipated by the platform designer—and, of course, also in ways that are anticipated.

Anticipating the unanticipated is challenging, and this goal is a substantial portion of what makes platform development difficult.

Obviously, a platform designer cannot simply enumerate all possible combinations; the math is such that this takes too long. Successful platforms address this issue by placing an even greater emphasis on composition by standards. They must apply standards as constraints—because otherwise the building blocks won't fit together. And yet, they need to provide flexibility—because otherwise they won't enable interesting combinations. A substantial portion of platform design thus ends up being focused on this specific question of how to create composable yet rich interfaces.

Incrementalism

One way to think about the design process is as isomorphic to tree traversal. Each node in the tree is a larger problem that can be decomposed into child nodes, which must be visited in turn. Leaf nodes are the smaller problems that we solve directly, without further decomposition. The design can opt for breadth-first or depth-first traversal, but either way, the process is complete when all nodes have been visited.

Of course, such a linear approach would make software development quite slow. This approach might be acceptable, or even necessary, when a single individual tackles a project of modest size. However, most product development efforts will want to both move more quickly and deliver intermediate results along the way.

Intermediate results are accessed by working incrementally. The underlying notion is that you decompose and solve some of the problems, but not all of them, before you put the system back together in working form. Later increments can then return to any node in the tree and expand it further.

Incremental design is useful in a couple of different ways. First, it can address impatience: It's no fun—and sometimes demotivating—to wait too long to see something working. When I'm working on solo projects, I lean heavily into iterative design for this reason alone. It's satisfying to see each stage of work come to life, and it creates motivation to move on to the next incremental challenge.

Second, incrementalism is helpful when the desired endpoint is unclear or unknown. Maybe you know some of the problems to solve but not all of them, or you know all the problems but can't solve every one of them yet. Separate out the parts you do understand and get them working. Use the feedback from those results to inform later results.

One interesting result of working incrementally is that you sometimes find the later increments aren't needed at all. They might have seemed logical or necessary parts of the product when considered in the abstract. However, once the first increments are running, you may find those elements are sufficient—and the additional effort required to complete the later stages isn't worthwhile.

You can use this observation to avoid arguments over scope. Perhaps some members of the team think a full implementation is required; perhaps others think a minimal approach will suffice. Instead of debating the scope in the abstract, get both parties to agree to an incremental plan. Then check in after each increment is delivered. With results in hands, the two sides are more likely to find common ground.

Parallelism

Incrementalism organizes work over time; parallelism organizes work over people. The occasional solo project aside, most systems are developed by teams. The more independently the individuals on those teams can work, the more efficiently the work can proceed.

Fortunately, parallelism and decomposition go together [6]. Each subproblem, if well defined, represents a separate piece of work to be distributed to a different portion of the team. How well this operates in practice does depend on the decomposition. The more separable the pieces are and the cleaner the interfaces between them, the better this approach will work.

Generally, parallelism is more accessible at the upper layers of the system decomposition. For example, with a cloud-based product, the separation between the web application and the services is a clear opportunity to assign separate teams to each. This approach has the added advantage that the two elements of the decomposition may require different skills or technical knowledge, and the teams can be organized around these needs as well.

For parallelism to be worthwhile, the work to be done in isolation must outweigh the overhead of coordinating the interfaces and connections between these pieces. As the process of decomposition moves down the stack from applications or services to classes and methods, this ratio grows smaller. At the level of an individual class, applying parallelism to decomposition probably isn't worthwhile.

Interestingly, the conversations and coordination forced by parallelism can also be used to evaluate the design. For example, suppose a decomposition calls for a product to be implemented as three services—let's call them A, B, and C—and a team is assigned to each service. If the teams for A and C don't require much coordination, and neither do the teams for A and B, that's a positive sign that the decomposition is working well. It has created clean interfaces between the services, and the teams can work in parallel with minimal overhead.

However, perhaps the teams for B and C find themselves in constant conversations. Maybe they're meeting daily to address the number of issues arising, and the interface between those two services changes daily. That's a clear sign that the decomposition between B and C isn't working! What might not have been clear from the written design can become radically apparent in the team behaviors. This information should be used to revisit the design.

Organizational Structure

Many in the software industry are familiar with Conway's law [7], which states

> *Organizations which design systems ... are constrained to produce designs which are copies of the communication structures of these organizations.*

Generally, this observation is understood to describe a flow from the organization's structure to the software design. In the classical example, a system is decomposed into n elements because the organization was structured into n teams and, well, each team needed something to do, didn't it?

Although the law is accurate, Conway himself observed that it is, in fact, "a criterion for the structing of design organizations." This realization transforms it from an unhelpful excuse for poor designs into a useful tool. Do you want to reduce coupling between different elements of your system—perhaps so they can be independently reused? Then assign them to two different teams. It's even better if the two teams don't cooperate much.

Conversely, perhaps a design includes a complex component that will take substantial effort to realize but must have a uniform interface and behavior. It may be tempting to decompose it further and parcel out the work, but this approach will inevitably undermine the cohesiveness of the result. In such a case, it's better to staff up a single team, allocate more time for the team, or both.

The key here is to use the organization's structure as a tool. Use decomposition and the software design process to determine how the product should be structured. Then, structure your organization accordingly. You will get a system that copies the organization's structure—and that will be exactly what you wanted to get.

Work in the Open

The design process requires feedback, and feedback requires communication. We tell others about our work, and we seek responses that affirm the development of a shared understanding. When you communicate with your stakeholders, you receive a steady stream of information that embodies a wide variety of views. No two people will look at the system the same way, from the same point of view, or with the same knowledge and background.

Our own understanding of our design will inevitably evolve during these conversations. Depending on what we hear, we might realize that we are unclear in our explanations, thus leading us to find better explanations. Or we might not hear much at all, indicating that we need to invest more in communication. A successful conversation leads to change, whether that is in your communication, your design, or both. The sooner you can start these conversations, the better.

For this reason, you should strive to work in the open. By "working in the open," I mean that change proposals and other artifacts that record your work should be accessible to as many people as possible.

When you work in the open, a couple of important things happen. First, you avoid surprising your stakeholders late in the process with a design that they don't understand or agree with. I know it can be tempting to present others with a complete and compelling vision, but what feels to you like a triumph may feel to them like a fait accompli. Even if the work is great, your stakeholders may be aggrieved at the missed opportunity to participate.

The most interesting things we can hear are the questions and comments that uncover something new. No design is perfect, and every design can get better. When you're close to a design, and especially when you've designed it yourself, seeing these flaws and opportunities can be difficult.

Working in the open means you've shared earlier—and received feedback earlier. Note that the goal here is not to inform every reviewer of every change, and certainly not to have them review and provide feedback on every draft. Some of your readers—especially those less invested in the outcome—will wait until the work is more complete, and that's okay.

If you work in the open as a matter of course, the people who are invested and curious—whether about a specific issue or just in general—will know that they can participate, and they'll feel welcome in doing so. These people will find new drafts as they're published, and they'll invest time in reviewing them. For an architect, having early and eager reviews is a gift.

The second big thing that happens when you work in the open is that you reduce your own lock-in to what you've developed so far.

We're often strongly attached to whatever approach we take first, but few of us are so talented that we can't improve on that first idea. The longer you work on that first idea in isolation, the greater the risk that you'll get "stuck" on it, without exploring alternatives.

A disciplined architecture team will strive to avoid this outcome by developing multiple conceptual approaches earlier in the process. That helps, but even then a choice must be made among the alternatives. What better way to debate the merits of the alternatives than with peers who can help evaluate, question, and ideate? In my experience, very few designs fail to be improved when they are subjected to scrutiny.

The sooner you share and get feedback, the less risk you face of getting stuck on a first idea, and the sooner you'll get the feedback you need to improve the work. And when you do reach a complete design, you'll already have a group of reviewers who understand the proposal in depth.

Now, none of this means that every piece of feedback is correct. Each comment deserves a fair shake, but you may hear plenty that you don't want to act on. That's fine, so long as it's justified. After all, some of these ideas you receive will be bad ideas! You're not here to please your reviewers; your goal is to create a great design.

But don't forget that you are also striving for dialogue and shared understanding. From that point of view, every piece of feedback tells you something. Was the comment based on a misunderstanding of what you wrote? Possibly that misinterpretation is on the reviewer, but it may also be a signal that your explanation is not as clear as it needs to be. If you can fix it, you'll save later readers the same trouble.

Some feedback may suggest perfectly reasonable alternatives, but alternatives that you won't adopt. In the spirit of creating a dialogue, these deserve a response. Avoid the temptation to pen a defense; these alternatives are not threats. Simply explain your criteria for the decision you made, whatever it is. In addition, document the explanation for the next reader who wonders anew if the same alternative was considered.

It's been my experience that learning to work in the open can be difficult for some people. If you conceive of your skill as an architect as purely equivalent to the quality of your own designs, then all feed-back is fraught with peril, but feedback received early, on possibly half-baked ideas, especially so. Each comment will feel like a criticism, and you'll wish you'd had the chance to address it before anyone else saw your "mistake."

This view, however, is not how one should approach the design process. Architectural design, like the rest of product development, is a team effort. An architect's job is to deliver a suitable design using all available resources, including input from peers, stakeholders, and so on. This approach will inevitably involve incorporating insights and feedback from others. Doing so makes the design stronger, so this kind of thoughtful criticism should be welcomed.

If you struggle with this—or see others who do—remember that you are not your work. It seems easy to lose track of this distinction at times. People often identify strongly with what they create, and they confuse praise and criticism of one with the other. Working in the open doesn't make this easier, but it does put the issue front and center. And the more we can learn to separate ourselves from our work—and therefore act objectively on it—the better our work will be.

Giving Up

Not all designs will pan out. If a design cannot be realized under the parameters set by the original change proposal, then it should be abandoned, and the work returned to an earlier stage. Use what you've learned during the design phase to revisit this proposal, and the rejected alternatives. Armed with new information, you can revisit that decision and, if warranted, proceed down a different path.

Giving up and starting over can be hard to do because, as noted earlier, people get attached to the designs in which they're invested. That, in turn, can lead to long, drawn-out discussions about whether to reconsider earlier alternatives. These debates confuse project con-cerns, such as timelines, with engineering concerns, such as viability.

That makes them difficult to resolve and unlikely to produce good outcomes.

You can avoid these quagmires by making the return to the change proposal phase automatic. For example, you might set a rule that this step is required if the estimate for the design's delivery slips by more than some number of weeks. Stop work on the design and bring the team's attention back to the conceptual stage. Ask if there are new, alternative proposals that should be added to the evaluation. Then decide to switch gears or—as can happen—recommit to the original approach.

Abandoning a design can seem disruptive and will almost certainly result in delays. Resist the urge to push through in hopes of keeping to the schedule. It is nearly always better to take a short, predictable delay than to let such issues fester. When they fester, they tend to cause more trouble and bigger delays later. And if you have built an effective process for evaluating and selecting change proposals, reassessing the situation at hand should not take long.

Done

Once a design is done, it should not be changed. It can be superseded by some subsequent change proposal, of course. That change proposal, however, must be evaluated in the context of the system's current state, considering the already-completed design work.

Projects should put each additional change through the same level of rigor used to review and approve the original design. The goal here isn't to reduce change through a burdensome process. The point is that you should apply the same level of rigor to the change as you did to the original design. Whether that's a heavyweight or lightweight process is up to the project.

Architects sometimes find this difficult! As implementation of a design proceeds, they may think of new and better ways to approach the design. It can be hard to set those shiny possibilities aside and stick with the plan of record. Nonetheless, teams that master this ability will do better at shipping software on time. The ability to make decisions in a disciplined fashion—and then stick with them—is a sign of the team's maturity.

Summary

Design is the third stage of change, and the time at which we work out the details of a conceptual change. Simple changes can taken on directly, but even for the simplest of changes, architects should seek feedback by working in the open.

For more complex changes, one can apply the design process illustrated in Figure 5.1.

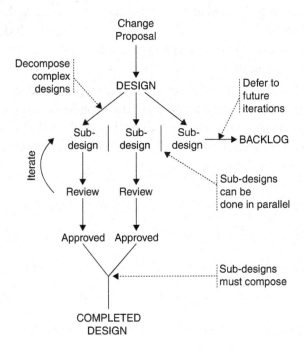

Figure 5.1
An illustration of paths through the design process.

If the design is complex, it should be decomposed into smaller problems. This can be done recursively—forming a tree of designs—until each sub-design is manageable on its own.

Depending on the nature of the change, it may be possible to take on these sub-designs incrementally, completing one before moving on to the next. An incremental approach can help demonstrate progress and lead to early feedback. Sometimes, later increments become unnecessary, or can be postponed for some time. Postponed items are returned to the architectural backlog.

If the decomposition allows for it and the team has capacity, these sub-design efforts can also proceed in parallel. Parallelized work should be aligned with organizational boundaries, but most is also informed by the coupling between different sub-designs. Finding the right balance might involve changes to your design or to your organization.

Work should be done in the open, so that the team members receive feedback early and often. When sub-designs are completed, a check must be performed to ensure that the composition of those sub-designs fulfills the original design requirements. Once this is done, the design is complete. Further changes should be handled as new change proposals, starting at the beginning of the process.

Throughout the process, teams should keep in mind that not all designs will be completed. Some will be abandoned as not worthwhile; others may be abandoned because they don't work out. A strong change process identifies these situations as early as possible, rather than focusing on delivering every change.

Chapter 6

Decisions

Running a software architecture practice, as well as building a product, running a team, making a change, and fixing a defect, are all activities that involve a never-ending series of decisions. Ultimately, the product we deliver is the accumulation of changes we decided to make—and the ones we decided not to make. A strong decision-making capability is thus an essential part of the process for an effective software architecture practice.

The more effectively and efficiently we make these decisions, the better and more quickly we deliver. Instead of letting each decision just happen in some ad-hoc fashion, we can put a structured, repeatable process in place. In doing so, we can also develop our decision-making skills. We can create predictability and velocity in arriving at a decision, and we can reduce the number of decisions with poor outcomes or that need to be revisited.

When we think about decisions one by one, we tend to focus on inputs and outputs. Inputs are the facts or opinions we have at hand; they are the variables that we can weigh as we consider our options. Outputs are the results of the decision—such as whether a decision will produce a better product, accelerate a delivery schedule, and so on. From this vantage point, every decision is unique.

From another vantage point, we can focus on what stays the same from one decision to the next. The actual inputs and outputs always vary, but every decision has inputs and outputs. They all involve people who make, approve, contribute to, or are informed of the decision. And they proceed according to a process and a timeline.

When addressing the decision-making process, there's often a temptation to adopt or create a framework that provides a relatively rigid, structured, and documented approach to the process. A heavy-weight process is fine for the small number of broad and critical decisions that need to be made, but these are few and far between. Most decisions are relatively small—it's not their individual outcomes but their accumulated outcomes that carry weight.

The real challenge in developing decision-making skills, then, is how decision-making scales *down* to the dozens of decisions made every day by everyone on the team. When dealing with many small decisions, a rigorous process that requires documentation, tracking, meetings, and notifications does more harm than good, and it won't be followed. A scaled-down decision-making process should require nothing more than recognition that a decision is being made and easy-to-follow guidance.

The bulk of this chapter consists of a set of questions designed to provide such guidance. Teams and individuals can quickly ask these questions about each decision they face, large and small. Their answers will help identify when it's time to move ahead with a decision, and which decisions require more time and attention.

Will More Information Help?

No good decision can be made without reasonably complete information, but plenty of decisions are deferred too long while seeking further information that isn't relevant or has no impact. Thus, the question to ask when deciding is not *Do we have all the information?* but rather *Do we have enough of it?*

It can help to ask this question explicitly. You may have gathered information from various contributors, but it can be hard to know if they've told you the whole story. Maybe they interpreted your question narrowly. Perhaps they avoided sharing additional information because you didn't ask, it seemed like more trouble, or they weren't sure if it was relevant. Perhaps it simply didn't come to mind.

If you ask your contributors what else you need to know, you create the space for them to share their additional knowledge—something they may have been reluctant to do uninvited. You may also shake loose some additional information that hasn't yet come to mind. Show appreciation for whatever they come up with—it may not be helpful for this decision, but you may need them to volunteer their knowledge again and a negative response might dampen future helpfulness.

If you're still not sure if you have all the information you need, ask yourself what information would change your decision—or give you greater certainty—if you had it. Then check whether you have that information or need to track it down.

And then stop. Once you've checked in with your contributors and yourself, decide. Further information gathering, because it's no longer focused, is unlikely to result in much, if any, relevant information.

For example, imagine your system has a "uses" dependency from Service A on Service B; that is, Service A depends on Service B to do some work, realized as a request or message sent from A to B. You've recently realized that this dependency is questionable:

- Service A invokes Service B for only one operation; let's call it F().
- Maintaining F() in Service B is expensive because it requires coordination between the Service A and Service B teams.

A change proposal has been put forward to remove the "uses" dependency of Service A on Service B, to be accomplished by moving operation F() out of Service B and into Service A. The decision to be made is whether to proceed.

Given only the facts presented here, there is additional information that's material to making this decision. For example, you'll want to know:

- Does this change create a new dependency between Service A and some other service? If F() is self-contained, probably not. However, if F() has its own dependencies, then the answer will depend on which services it uses, and whether Service A already uses them.

- Does the addition or removal of any such dependencies align with or violate any relationship constraints in the system's architecture?

Other information could be gathered but isn't material to the decision. Why was F() in Service B to begin with? Did F() have some other use in the past? Might F() be used by more services in the future? Will we create a new dependency from Service A to Service B in the future? Any of these questions will give you more information, but they won't help you decide. If anything, they'll complicate the decision by bringing immaterial and speculative information into the discussion.

When making a decision, focus on getting just enough information and no more. Having enough information helps you make good decisions that don't get reversed. Not gathering excess information keeps the decision-making process moving ahead.

What's Happening in the Meantime?

Decisions take time. Possibly not very much, but no decision is instantaneous. We can be tempted to draw them out for a variety of reasons. Sometimes, the decision itself doesn't seem important, and this tends to detract from the urgency of making it. We might also delay because we need more information or we're simply having trouble choosing between alternatives.

In the meantime, the status quo persists. As decision makers, we must be aware of this fact and take it into account in our decision-making process. If the decision you're considering affects only an isolated portion of the system with no active development, you can likely afford to take your time. What's happening in the meantime isn't going to impact, or be impacted by, your decision.

But suppose you're still deciding whether to move F() from Service B to Service A. Furthermore, several other teams are working on changes that require using operation F(). Because F() is currently in

Service B, that means these other teams are implementing a dependency on and integrating with Service B.

The timeliness of your decision will have a big impact on that work:

- If you decide quickly to move F() from Service B to Service A, you'll have some impact on the other work, but the sooner you make that decision, the smaller that impact will be.
- If you decide to move F() but only after taking more time to think it over, you'll create more work. While you were making up your mind, those other teams already integrated their changes with Service B. Now the change that moves F() got more expensive, because F() has more callers.
- If you abandon the change, then the other teams can proceed, and no new work is required. However, the Service A and Service B teams need to continue to coordinate.

When considering a decision, remember that you're deciding in parallel with a system that is undergoing constant change. If your decision impacts or is impacted by parallel work, take that into account. The more quickly you can decide, the less likely that decision is to be disrupted by changing facts on the ground and the less likely it becomes that something unfortunate happens in the meantime.

How Many Decisions Are in Play?

Decisions don't always present themselves in the simplest possible form. What seems like a single decision might, in fact, be better handled as more than one. For example, consider a data loss defect discovered in a production system. Clearly, a decision needs to be made as to how to fix the defect. However, that may take some time, and in the meantime the risk of data loss remains. In such a situation, how to temporarily negate the risk (i.e., by disabling a feature) and how to permanently address the risk (i.e., by fixing the defect) might be taken as two separate decisions.

Conversely, what appears to be two separate decisions may actually be just one. Returning to an example from Chapter 5, suppose that two different service teams are both considering how to add full text search support to the records they store. That might appear to be two separate decisions, to be taken separately by each team. A better take might be that it's a single decision about how to support full text search for all records stored by the system. By viewing it as a single decision, the team creates space to consider creating a new architectural component that provides search capabilities for both dependent services.

At the same time, whether to provide a unified search capability and which technology to use for that capability are, again, two separate decisions. One cannot reasonably decide to adopt a unified search capability without knowing that there's at least one viable implementation option. But if there are multiple implementation options, selecting which one as part of the same decision will overload the decision-making process and slow things down. In the meantime, teams might implement their own full-text search, which is the opposite of the desired outcome.

Architects, because their view is system-wide, are well positioned to help clarify the number of decisions to be made, as well as the dependencies between them. At the same time, that tendency to see the "big picture" can make it tempting to lump together multiple decisions. An effective software architecture team will avoid this trap, instead identifying and making a series of discrete decisions. They will also communicate clearly and consistently about the number and scope of each decision as they proceed.

What's the Cost of Not Doing It?

When evaluating a change, we're making a choice between sticking with the system as it is today versus making that change. On the one hand, the cost of making the change is, other things being equal, relatively easy to estimate. Sticking with the status quo, on the other hand, often seems "free." After all, how can not changing anything have a cost?

Of course, nearly all systems have an ongoing cost. Even a system not undergoing new investment requires maintenance. Vulnerabilities may demand a response. And in the world of cloud computing, compute, network, and storage costs are all ongoing.

Remember that component someone wrote in a new (but esoteric) language because, they said, they just wanted to try it out? Well, that engineer left, and now we're stuck maintaining that component in a language that none of the current team members knows. Most of the time it just works, but now and then it needs a fix or an upgrade. Those changes are expensive because, each time they arise, someone learns just enough about this esoteric language to fix the issue—we think?— and then we check in the code and try to forget about it.

Now someone has proposed rewriting that component in our preferred programming language. Rewriting seems expensive because the costs are incurred all at once as a lump sum. The ongoing costs of maintaining that component, in contrast, are spread out over time in dribs and drabs, which makes them hard to account for. As humans, our intuition is to avoid things that are significant, one-time expenses. We struggle to compare one-time costs with ongoing costs. It's a blind spot where intuition doesn't serve us well.

If you did add up the ongoing costs, you might well find that it's a net win to rewrite that component. True, it's an upfront cost. But once it's done, it's done. Issues may still arise in that component from time to time, but now they are no more costly to address than anything else in the system. The simplification of removing the additional language will also pay further dividends.

To be clear, the point of asking this question is not that we should decide to make more changes than we do. Not every change will reduce the ongoing maintenance or operational costs of the system—and that likely isn't the goal of most changes that we will consider. Rather, the point is that people often focus too much on immediate costs versus ongoing costs. Asking ourselves about ongoing costs can help mitigate this behavior.

Can I Live with This Change?

Often, we're deciding not whether to make a change but which change to make. These decisions often involve trade-offs between immediate speed and *quality*, where quality is a subjective measure of various attributes of the proposed change. For example, a change that adds a special case to the system might be judged as "lower quality" than one that adds a new, more general behavior.

When these decisions arise, it is tempting to compromise by deciding to make the fast-but-lower-quality change now and the expensive-but-better change later. The obvious problem with such compromises is that you're committing the team to more total work than either change alone would require. I have never encountered a project team that *wanted* to do something twice, when it really needed to be done only once.

Of course, the point of the compromise is that it gets something done sooner (the fast part) while still promising a high-quality implementation in the long run (the slow but better part). In theory, that will satisfy both sides of the debate. But it doesn't work.

It doesn't work because *teams cannot commit themselves to future work*. Product development teams always have new claims on their resources—an endless stream of new features to write, new technologies to adopt, defects to fix, optimizations to make. Any expensive-but-better thing promised for later will always and inevitably be competing for resources against this other work. Most of the time, that other work will be legitimately more important—especially when your first change is already made.

That doesn't mean you can't decide to use the fast-but-lower-quality approach. What it does mean is that *you must be willing to live with the change*. If you pick the fast-but-lower-quality approach, you must be willing to accept that there may always be other, more important things to do than revisit it—and so you will live with it forever. And if you can do that, then you probably didn't need the expensive-but-better option anyway.

Architecture teams often seem to find this question especially difficult, perhaps because expensive-but-better options appeal to their desire to deliver quality work. The higher-quality work may be more elegant, or more innovative, or simply instill more pride in its creator. That may lead architects to double down on the expensive option, and even to refuse help with the cheap-but-less-desirable approach. Leaders may be tempted to "buy them off" by promising to revisit the situation later—even though such promises cannot be kept.

To avoid this situation, emphasize that the architects, too, will have to live with whatever decision is made. While it may be disappointing to forgo the expensive-but-better option, the available opportunity is to improve the fast-but-lower-quality option to achieve something that, while perhaps a bit costlier, will be fit-for-purpose. In other words, architects should strive to find the moderately-expensive-and-we-can-live-with-it design that lies between the extremes. An effective software architecture team makes decisions that everyone can live with because they fall within the resource and time constraints, without undermining the integrity of the system.

Technical Debt

Deciding on a low-quality change is often described as taking on "technical debt." By analogy, a superseding, high-quality change pays off technical debt. Teams can keep track of how much debt they've taken on. In theory, technical debt is an accounting mechanism for the promises made to "fix it later."

Unfortunately, the analogy with financial debt is deeply misleading. When you take on "good debt," such as a small business loan, you are making an investment that is expected to generate a return—income that will be used to repay that debt later. You're doing things such as purchasing equipment or hiring people—things that increase the value of your business.

That's the opposite of how technical debt accounting works. When you take on technical debt, you're not borrowing to make an investment; you're just adding up how much you under-invested via a low-quality implementation. And whereas investments generate returns, poor implementations create additional ongoing expenses due to increased maintenance, operating costs, outages, and defects. That makes it harder, not easier, to pay off the debt later.

> If debt is the right analogy, then technical debt is the vacation you couldn't afford but charged to your credit card anyway. Some people who can't manage their spending do eventually pay off their credit card debt—but many others declare bankruptcy.

What Is the Cost of Getting This Wrong?

When faced with a decision, it's tempting to think it's necessary to arrive at the right outcome. In fact, we often assume that there is a right outcome—just one of them. In practice, this is rarely the case.

Outcomes may be better or worse, of course. In many cases, however, they are simply different. This issue often arises when discussing naming of properties, classes, services, and so on. Naming is important. But naming isn't a mathematical equation with one correct answer. Names that mislead are poor choices, to be sure. But when two names are indistinguishable alternatives, often we have several reasonable choices available to us. The cost of picking the "wrong" one is zero when the "right" one is an equally good alternative.

The second problem with the right-versus-wrong framing is that it ignores the longevity of the outcome. Of course, some decisions are hard to change. The primary programming language of an application comes to mind; such a decision is rarely changed, and typically, we live with the decision indefinitely.

But most decisions are narrower in scope and made in evolving systems. When a decision can or will be revisited, we should spend much less time on it. Over-investing in a decision that has a lifetime of weeks or can be readily changed isn't a good use of time and energy that can be spent elsewhere.

Once we realize this, we can frame right-versus-wrong in another way: What's the consequence if we do choose the wrong answer? If it's an easy fix, then we may be better off making a quick decision and correcting course later if needed. In fact, for a decision with a low cost of change and high uncertainty, simply proceeding in one direction can be cheaper than making a better decision, even if the decision is changed later.

An effective software architecture team thinks about the cost of getting a decision wrong and doesn't over-invest in decisions that are readily corrected. They preserve their time and energy for the decisions that are truly expensive to change.

How Much More Certain Can I Be?

Having worked your way this far through the decision-making checklist, you may find yourself still less than entirely certain about the outcome. Perhaps you have some time to make the decision; you're not worried about what's happening in the meantime. You've gathered a lot of information, but it's not definitive. And you have a couple of options on the table, neither of which looks great but both of which you'll have to live with for a long time. This scenario does happen, and it can be a real quagmire for decision making.

At this point, you must ask yourself whether additional certainty is available. Would more time, information, options, or analysis help? Typically, each of these activities demonstrates diminishing returns. You'll arrive at most of your certainty early in the decision-making process. Dragging things out may help a bit, but you'll never get to 100% for anything but the most trivial issues.

The truth is that decisions are always made with incomplete knowledge and less than absolute certainty. You may believe that you have all the information, but it's more likely that you don't know what you don't know. It's uncomfortable to decide something when we recognize our remaining uncertainty, know that we might be wrong, and realize that we may have to revisit it later. Our best response is not to strive for total certainty, but rather to recognize that complete certainty isn't achievable. No one likes this, but if the decision is your responsibility, you need to make it and move on while accepting those risks.

Now, this is not a license to make rash, quick, or ill-informed decisions. Waiting will sometimes bring new information to light; time to ponder a decision will sometimes lead to clarity that is absent early on. If you are substantially uncertain about a decision, you should probably seek the time, information, or analysis required to change that. Proceeding with uncertainty isn't about rash judgment; it's about recognizing that absolute certainty is never achieved.

Is This My Decision to Make?

Until now, this chapter has focused on questions that help guide the decision-making process and can be applied by anyone deciding something. They ask about issues that might prevent an individual from deciding. One way or another, those barriers need to be dealt with and a decision made.

But before deciding, you must also ask if the decision is yours to make. Ideally, lines of responsibility and good job descriptions will make this answer crystal clear. If you ever find a job like that, please let me know—I'd like to apply.

As architects, decisions related to standards, principles, and other architectural concerns are our responsibility and, for the most part, should be ours to make. We receive inputs—for example, in the form of requirements—that constrain the decisions we make, but how we address those requirements is up to us.

However, some decisions have implications beyond architecture. For example, we might want to use third-party services or software. This will often bring up contractual and monetary concerns. That doesn't mean such approaches shouldn't be considered, but it does mean pulling a different set of decision makers into the room.

When facing a decision that has broader implications and therefore involves more stakeholders, consider whether you should apply a formal decision-making framework. On the one hand, as discussed earlier, such frameworks impose too much overhead for small decisions. On the other hand, the structure they impose is designed to deal with complex decisions that involve complex trade-offs and different points of view.

For example, some organizations use some form of a *responsibility assignment matrix* to identify participants, and their roles, in significant decisions. If a decision is yours to make, then you are in the "approver" or "accountable" role. If you are driving a decision but someone else is the approver, then you are the "recommender" or "driver." Depending on the specific approach used, the matrix may include other roles, including consulted, informed, review required, input required, sign-off required, and so on.

Although some decisions need to be escalated, other decisions should be delegated. If you are architecturally accountable for a subsystem, can this decision be made by the owner of a specific service or library? If you are responsible for a library, can this decision be made by an engineer working on the class or function in question? Finding these opportunities to delegate has advantages.

The first advantage of delegation is that it frees up your time. Most likely you have a lot of work to do. You have designs to create and decisions that only you can make. When you find something that can be delegated, it's an opportunity to take something off your plate and create space for all that other stuff.

Delegation is also an opportunity for others on the team. Maybe that service lead is relatively junior; the chance to assess and make these calls can be a learning experience for them. When you delegate this work, don't just hand it off. Provide some context. Explain why you're delegating to them. Make yourself available to help guide them as they take on the work, should they need it. And then let them own it.

Of course, these two modes—escalating up, delegating down—are related. One day you may escalate an issue to an executive; the next day an engineer may escalate an issue to you, as architect. Teams that have practice moving decisions to the correct level will ultimately produce better decisions.

Am I Aligned?

Some decisions are "big." They involve many stakeholders. They will impact the work of hundreds or thousands of people. They will drive product revenue—whether up or down. They commit companies and organizations to long-term investments or partnerships. The scope of such decisions makes them important, but it also makes them *visible*. Everyone can see that they are being made, even if they might disagree on whether the decisions are being made well.

The software development process encompasses innumerable decisions. Thousands upon thousands of decisions must be made, on everything: architectural principles, subsystem boundaries, function names, invariants in "for" loops. These decisions lie at the core of the engineering process; they are how engineering happens.

Clearly, most of these decisions are not "big" decisions. No one needs to gather stakeholders and draft proposals to assess the use of a "for" loop versus a "do-while" loop. But for big decisions—those with significant impact—we can and should invest in careful and deliberate decision making. In essence, the investment in making the decision should correspond to its impact. A team that spends too much time on small decisions will move far too slowly while, in the meantime, other things happen.

The questions in this chapter are designed to operate at these different scales. For the smallest decisions, these questions can be answered quickly, on the spot, without consultation. If they can't be answered quickly, that's an indication the decision has a bigger impact, and a prompt to give the decision its due consideration.

And yet, the many, many small decisions, made quickly and without consultation, will, in aggregate, have a big impact. It cannot be otherwise: Those decisions sit between the "big" decisions and the algorithms, code, and data structures that manifest the product.

Given this reality, every decision, no matter how small, should be made in alignment with your architectural principles and technical vision. It's this alignment that guarantees the thousands of local decisions, in aggregate, work together toward the product's goals, rather than against those goals or against each other. Before you make any decision, ask if it's aligned with the product's architectural principles and vision.

Can I Document It?

In my experience, nothing brings clarity to a decision like trying to document it. More than once something that seemed clear as I was thinking it through fell apart as I wrote it down. If you're not able to clearly document a decision, that's a strong sign that you haven't yet made a clear and coherent decision.

Indeed, thinking about documenting a decision *before* it's made, rather than after, will help prompt answers to many of the concerns and questions that you need to address. Starting a draft of that document early provides the perfect place to work out your thoughts as you proceed.

That said, I recommend against the overuse of *decision documents*—that is, documents that exist solely to capture the decision. Whenever possible, document your decision as part of some larger artifact: a change proposal, an architectural specification, a design document, a vision paper, or even comments in your code. Reserve decision documents for the rarer circumstances in which decisions cannot be packaged with one of these items.

This advice is primarily practical. Teams make innumerable decisions, from small to large. It would clearly be impractical to impose the overhead of a separate decision document for every one of those decisions. If some other artifact, be it code or documentation, already captures the context, the decision, and the stakeholders, there's no need and little value in creating a separate decision document.

For example, Chapter 5 introduced *change proposals* as a mechanism through which architecture teams can propose, evaluate, and decide which changes to make. A change proposal is more than just a decision record because it documents the proposal, relevant context, stakeholders, considerations, and so on. But it can also document the decision: Ultimately, each proposal is either approved or rejected. A separate decision document would have nothing to add. If you organize your architectural work around change proposals (from Chapter 4) and follow the practices discussed in Chapter 7, you'll rarely, if ever, find a need for separate decision documents.

Architectural Decision Records

Some teams make a practice of using architectural decision records (ADRs) [8], and that set of ADRs forms the architectural documentation for the system. ADRs share some similarities with change proposals, which were introduced in Chapter 4. However, ADRs emphasize documentation for decisions that have been made, whereas change proposals emphasize experimentation with potential changes.

When teams rely only on ADRs, they trade off convenience for the author of that record, who now must document the decision, against that of their readers. Readers, to understand the system's architecture, must now read through all the ADRs to understand how any of the system works. Worse, some of the later decisions might override the earlier decisions, and each reader must work that out for themselves. It's the equivalent of trying to read source code by looking at the changes committed to a source code repository one-by-one instead of reading the current version of the code with those changes applied.

Documentation should always be optimized for the reader; there are many, many more readers than authors. If your team uses ADRs, be sure that you also update the system's specifications after each decision. As with change proposals, you'll know you are doing this properly if no one ever needs to consult them once they are recorded.

Summary

Decision making happens all the time, and not just in architecture. As part of our jobs, we tend to focus on the facts. However, like any repeatable process, paying attention to the process can help us get better at it. To be good at decision making is its own skill, and one that can be nurtured and developed.

A relatively small number of big decisions merit a more formalized process than what's described here. They might be individually tracked and require documentation and formal approval. Most decisions, however, neither warrant nor receive this kind of scrutiny. The questions offered here can quickly be applied to every decision. Keep them in mind.

Chapter 7
Practices

Software architecture may be an inescapably abstract pursuit, but it does not turn abstract thought directly into code. A smoothly operating architecture practice turns thought into code via a set of tools and processes that, along the way, produce an array of intermediate artifacts. These artifacts help architects perform their job, help architecture teams manage their activities, and facilitate coordination and communication with other functions, organizations, and leaders.

This chapter describes these essential architectural practices and explores how they function. These practices support the change, design, and decision-making activities discussed in preceding chapters, as well as introduce some new aspects and behaviors that they enable. Chapter 8 offers further guidance on creating, organizing, and using many of these artifacts.

Tools are referenced here only by function, and not by brand or vendor. The landscape of available tools continues to evolve, threatening to quickly make any specific recommendation obsolete. Different teams may also need to consider the availability of tools based on their industry, employer, jurisdiction, and more. In any case, you don't need to use any specific tool to be successful.

Leveraging the tools that are already available to your team is often the wiser course of action, especially if they are familiar both to your team and to your stakeholders. When an architecture team insists on a toolset that differs from the tools used by the product managers, engineers, and others they work with, they distance themselves from some of their most critical colleagues. That is not an argument for depriving your team of valuable working tools. However, if you adopt different tools, focus on those that offer meaningful differentiation.

Backlog

As explained in Chapter 4, architecture teams should maintain a record of current, past, and future work in the form of an architecture backlog. Structuring your backlog as a set of change proposals also simplifies the management of your process by aligning the two. Decisions to accept or reject a change proposal then correspond directly to backlog updates. Conversely, inspecting the backlog readily informs you of how many changes are under way, how many are pending, and so forth.

There's no ideal size or scope for change proposals because the changes themselves come in all shapes and sizes. A simple proposal might, for example, add a new, optional parameter to an existing API call. (That's still an architectural change if the API or parameter is governed by the architecture team.) A complex proposal might call for refactoring an existing service or adding a new subsystem. Later, we'll discuss processes that can scale according to the magnitude of the change. Regarding the backlog, the key is to capture each item.

Related proposals should be linked together. For example, perhaps you've generated three proposals, each proposing a different way of adding a new feature to your application. Selecting one implies rejecting the others. By maintaining those links in your backlog, you can readily see and manage the implications of each decision.

The backlog becomes even more effective if you model all your team's work as change proposals. Are you considering an update to your vision? Log a change proposal. Are you debating whether to adopt a new architectural principle? Log a change proposal. Are you thinking about switching the tools used to maintain your backlog? Log a change proposal. When you get into the habit of organizing all your work in this way, you can not only apply tools (such as the backlog) uniformly but also use your process and decision-making skills consistently.

It's in the nature of the human mind that, as we work our way through a change, related thoughts will occur to us. Some of these will be mundane connections; perhaps you realize it's getting late, and you've forgotten to take the trash out. Others will be relevant but distracting; you might realize that the issue you've just identified will also impact the next change you have to tackle. Sometimes, the connections will be surprising—those insights are the intrinsic creativity of the mind in action. Whether mundane or inspired, these connections can distract you from the task at hand.

A backlog is, of course, a mechanism for keeping track of what needs to be done, as well as selecting what needs to be done next. However, the best part of a backlog is often that it forms a collective, external memory bank. When new ideas crop up, add them to the backlog and forget them. Once an idea has been extracted from your mind and recorded in the backlog, it can be set aside, and your focus can return to the task at hand. That's the power of a backlog as memory: It lets the team forget about things—at least for a while. Furthermore, it has perfect recall; human memory is decidedly more fallible.

A busy architecture team can easily have hundreds of items in its backlog, quietly staying out of the way while the team focuses on what's important. A suitable tool should enable the inclusion of at least this many items. To do that, it's ideal if each record has separate fields for priority, status, and other criteria by which you might want to search or sort the backlog. Issue tracking tools often work well for this purpose.

It's critical to capture clear descriptions of these items when they're recorded. We capture these items with the intention of coming back to them later, but we don't know if that will happen days, weeks, or months in the future. A quick note that fails to capture context and detail is an insufficient memory and might not be helpful when you come back to it later. This doesn't mean that every item needs a novel-length description, but a good paragraph will be much more useful than a brief sentence fragment.

As with any tool, teams must also develop the habit of using it. Everyone on the team will come up with items that should be on the list; this will happen all the time during the normal course of their work. People often like to talk about these when they come up—they might pop over to your desk to mention a new idea or send an email to the team. These interruptions can be redirected with a quick "Great idea—let's add it to the backlog."

By adding every item to the backlog, we both memorialize those items and defer the need to evaluate them. Whether you suspect the item is critically important or utterly irrelevant, add it to the backlog. You can return to it later when it can be judged critically and rationally, at a time when assessment is not clouded by the other concerns at hand.

Of course, for the backlog to be useful, it must be revisited periodically. This can happen first when you add a new backlog item. We should do "X," you are thinking—with some excitement—and immediately start adding this new item. Before you click to add it, spend a moment checking to see if "do X" is already on the list. (Here, basic search capabilities in whatever tool you use will help immensely.) If the item is already there, review it. Perhaps you can expand on the argument, revise the description, or add clarity. Regardless, preventing a duplicate entry helps keep the backlog tidy.

Items that have been previously considered and rejected should be kept in the backlog, too—don't delete them! If possible, use a tool that supports a "closed" or "resolved" state so that you can quickly distinguish what you've dispatched from what you've haven't. Maybe "do X" was raised last year and rejected. That doesn't mean the idea can't be revisited, but here you can use the collective, externalized memory of the team to help determine whether revisiting this subject is worthwhile—and if so, why.

The subset of backlog items that are actively under way should be updated as work progresses and reviewed regularly. Here a tool that tracks the status of each item is ideal. With accurate status information in hand, leaders can check in every week on the items in progress and see how they're coming along. Is a proposal almost complete? You might need to block time to review it. Is a proposal not reaching completion? Perhaps you need to check on the work to see what's disrupting progress. When items are actively being worked, teams can rely on this externalized memory to maintain awareness of day-to-day progress and changes.

You'll also want to keep track of the items that will be tackled next. Out of a backlog with hundreds of items in it, this need not be more than five to ten changes. If your project runs according to a larger planning cycle or maintains a roadmap, that may provide all the information you need to know which changes will come next. If not, you may need to invest in curating your next items once a month or so. Whatever approach you use, the goal is to be ready in advance to have architects move on to their next task when they're ready to pick it up.

Periodically, you need to perform a housecleaning sweep. I like to set aside some time with the team three or four times a year during which we review each item that isn't active or "up next." (We don't have to review the other items because we're already looking at them regularly.) As we review each item, we ask a set of questions:

- **Is this item still relevant?** Perhaps the system has evolved, or other decisions have made this item obsolete. It can be closed accordingly.
- **Do we want to address this now?** We recorded this item because we thought we'd want to address it someday; maybe that time has come, and we should move it to the "up next" list. Of course, there's a practical limit to how many items can be activated at any one time.
- **What other items relate to this one?** Although we should check for obvious duplicates as we add items to the list, these reviews often uncover clusters of related items—sometimes even from different sources. This is a chance to consolidate several items into one, or to link them together such that, should we return to one of them, we're also reminded of the others.

Conducting these periodic reviews also helps reinforce the understanding that filing an item on the list is not the same as consigning it to oblivion. Having confidence that these items will be revisited helps make the backlog mechanism work.

Another good time to consult this list is before planning exercises, whether those are strictly architectural or broader exercises for the product or platform. Planning cycles create an opportunity for the architecture team to identify work they need to get done and set time aside for it. If you've diligently captured these ideas in your external memory bank, they'll be ready and waiting when you need them.

Catalogs

A backlog is nothing more than a catalog of change proposals. Just as it's useful to catalog change proposals, it's useful for architecture teams to maintain catalogs of software components and data models.

Software catalogs record a system's components and their relationships. Depending on the type of system you're building, those components might be libraries, services, applications, frameworks, databases, and so on. At a minimum, each entry should capture metadata about the component, such as its type, technology dependencies, and relationship to other components. Links to documentation, responsible individuals, runbooks, and the like may also be relevant.

Data model catalogs record the data types, entity types, and relationships that describe the data on which a system operates. Depending on your system and the technologies it uses, these may be described in abstract data modeling languages, schemas, or format specifications.

Software and data model catalogs provide additional documentation on the current state of the system. That is, they augment any unstructured system documentation that supports the change process, documenting the system's current state.

Because these catalogs neither change as frequently as the backlog nor collect the same metadata, it's not necessary to use the same tool to create and maintain them as is used for your backlog. It is, however, ideal if you can maintain links between entries and their related change proposals. In many tools, entries have unique URLs, and maintaining these relationships can be as simple as recording that URL in related items.

Templates

An effective architecture team will spend the bulk of its time on changes. In turn, nothing has a greater potential impact on the team's productivity than its ability to complete changes efficiently.

Change proposals, including associated diagrams, should be captured in a written document. On large projects, teams may author hundreds or even thousands of these documents over just a few years' time. An approach that improves the efficiency of creating and approving these documents thus has a multiplicative effect on the team's productivity.

Structuring these documents according to a common template can accelerate every aspect of this process—not just writing and reviewing the documentation, but even creating and modifying the design itself. Templates accelerate writing by providing a structure for the author to follow. That avoids any unnecessary investment on the author's part in figuring out how to structure the documentation, freeing up the author's time and attention for documenting the design itself.

Templates offer similar advantages during the review process. Documents are read more often than they're written, so we want to optimize for the reviewer's time and effort. Furthermore, we want that effort focused on the work at hand—the design itself—and not on deciphering the structure or organization of the document. When each document adheres to the same format, it reduces the cognitive overhead imposed on the reviewer.

Most valuably, a good template acts as a checklist for the work itself. As they make their way through each section of the template, the author will "check off" each design aspect. A template should therefore prompt for each attribute that an architecture team expects. These can vary, but security, privacy, dependability, and other quality attributes are commonly found in these templates, and for just this reason.

Whether for the author or the reviewer, the consistency imposed by the template helps the structure fade into the background and brings the core details of the proposal itself to the fore. Here are the basic sections—the checklist items—that such a document should contain:

- **Status.** Anyone who's browsed a documentation repository and been unable to determine which documents are current, outdated, in progress, or abandoned will appreciate the need to accurately track and maintain status information. This section should appear right at the top so it can waive off any readers not interested in catching up on the designs abandoned five years ago.
- **Summary.** Every document should begin with a quick summary of the motivation and conceptual approach. In other words: What problem are we solving, and how are we solving it? A summary should be concise and complete; the rest of the document is "just the details."

The first two sections are all you need for a change that's still at the motivational or conceptual stage. The remaining sections should be considered when working through the detailed stage:

- **Terminology.** Don't bother documenting the project's existing terminology. (That should already be captured in the dictionary; see Chapter 8.) However, if a design introduces new terminology, then it should be defined here, before it's used later in the design.
- **Detailed Design.** This section provides the details and should be repeated for each major element of the design. For simple documents, a single instance will suffice, but a single document might contain up to perhaps half-a-dozen such sections. (If there is much more to cover, consider breaking the change up into multiple changes.)
- **Dependability.** Dependability is the umbrella term for a system's ability to address its reliability, resiliency, performance, scale, and related goals. In other words, it describes the extent to which a client can depend on a system to properly perform its function. This section should describe its level of dependability and how that is achieved.

- **Security and Privacy.** Architects must always and increasingly consider security, as well as applicable data protection and privacy concerns. This section should describe applicable concerns and indicate how they are addressed.
- **Efficiency.** Most relevant for cloud services, this section should examine the economics of the system at its anticipated scale. As use of the system grows, will the unit cost stay the same, increase, or decrease?
- **Compatibility.** Most documents will describe a change to an existing system, so the compatibility of those changes with existing software elements and data needs to be addressed. These concerns apply both within the system (where related changes and data migration may be feasible) and outside the system, including for clients that may depend on existing interfaces.
- **Impacts.** This section should summarize, in the form of a list or table, the components and other artifacts impacted by this change. Nothing new should be introduced in this section; it highlights and summarizes what's stated elsewhere so that this information is available at a glance.
- **Signatures.** Most documents will require approval of some sort, and it's been my experience that the best way to encourage an approver to take this responsibility seriously is to record their name in the document itself. It may not have the flair of John Hancock's signature, but it works.

When using the template, remember that it's a checklist. Perhaps your document won't have anything to say about compatibility. Maybe you're describing a new component, and compatibility concerns don't apply. A checklist is not a form; it doesn't require that you fill in every blank. The point of the checklist is to make you stop and think about each concern. If a given concern doesn't apply, so be it.

As noted earlier, changes vary vastly in scale. Your template should not impose an unnecessary burden on small changes. As a rule of thumb, a template should allow an architect to document a small, well-understood change in less than an hour. At the other end of the scale, the template should support designs with several major design elements.

Templates don't apply only to change proposals, although that's where they are likely to be most useful. You may also find them helpful for vision papers, catalog entries, and so on.

Consider your templates to be, in essence, standards maintained by your organization. First and foremost, their use should be a mandate—not an option. You don't get full benefit from a checklist or template if you use it only sometimes. If it's too burdensome to use it every time, fix the template.

Making the template a standard has one other benefit worth noting: The template becomes subject to the same change process that applies to everything else you do. If the template isn't working for someone, they should propose a change that addresses the issue. Log that proposal in your backlog and draft a revision to the standard—using the template, of course!

Reviews

Your change review process takes changes to their approved status. Or, occasionally, to rejection—an equally valid, if less satisfying, outcome. A predictable and effective review process helps support the team's overall efficiency.

The ability to develop a system's architecture is, obviously, an architect's core skill. However, I've come to view the ability to participate in a review as equally important. When working on a change, architects should be eager for reviews that will help improve and clarify the change and must be sufficiently humble to solicit and accept that feedback. As reviewers, architects can apply their skills, knowledge, and experience more broadly when they can share that feedback constructively. A review can't create a change, yet, without a review, a change is not at its best.

An effective review process combines four key ingredients: a common baseline, time to think, time to discuss, and diversity of thought.

To work from a common baseline means everyone involved in the review has the same understanding of the work, including the motivation and conceptual approach for a change. Common understanding is best achieved by working from a written description of the change. First, because writing it down—ideally using a template—encourages the author to be thorough and precise. Second, because only with a written document do we know that everyone is working from the same information. Standard, well-defined terminology further supports strong writing.

Once reviewers have the change proposal in hand, they need time to think about it. I recommend that the first part of the review process be conducted asynchronously—that is, not in a meeting. In many organizations, teams are spread across locations and time zones; an asynchronous process allows everyone to participate at a time that's convenient for them. Asynchronous reviews are also more comfortable for some participants because they can take more time to respond, rather than being put "on the spot" in a meeting.

Change proposals should be shared via a system, such as a wiki, that supports threaded comments and notifications. These are essential capabilities for asynchronous review and are widely available in a variety of tools; there's no need to go without them and, frankly, your review process won't work well without them. You can find the necessary capabilities in word processors, wikis, and source code repositories. And, while it would be silly to force everyone to comment on every change, the presence of well-reasoned comments is the best indicator that the document is lucid, and that reviewers have invested in understanding it.

The biggest challenge in running an asynchronous review is capturing and resolving each comment. To keep that as easy as possible, each comment should be contained in its own thread, and each thread should address only that one comment. Avoid the temptation to pile onto an existing thread, even if the feedback is related. These behaviors won't come naturally to all; be prepared to offer guidance on how to use commenting effectively to both authors and reviewers.

If the comment proposes a change and the author is agreeable, then the author should make the change and post a brief reply. The reviewer should confirm the change and, if it's acceptable, mark the comment as closed. I recommend an expiration time—perhaps five business days—after which the author can close the comment. The process cannot be at the mercy of busy reviewers.

If the proposed change is trivial and obvious—a typo, say—consider whether the reviewer has the option of making the change on their own. I prefer to use this rule because there's a lot of overhead in a comment thread to address something as trivial as a typo, and because it fosters a sense of shared ownership for the proposals. Ultimately, the proposal reflects on the author and the reviewer; no one wants it to contain typos or grammatical errors.

Other comments may be more difficult to resolve. Sometimes comments are off topic or out of scope. When that happens, capture the issue in your architectural backlog and mark the comment as resolved. The issue isn't resolved, of course, but the point here is to avoid burdening one proposal with other matters that will be resolved on a different timeline.

That leaves us with comments that represent significant disagreements between the author and the reviewer. If a comment thread goes beyond four or five total replies, that discussion should be moved outside the review process. Most likely, a review meeting should be held.

Holding a review meeting complements the asynchronous review with live discussion. Review meetings can serve two different purposes and, depending on how a review is proceeding, you might want to hold more than one to address these different challenges.

As just noted, the first reason to hold a review meeting is to deal with the situation in which the asynchronous review is struggling to resolve one or more issues. As valuable as asynchronous review processes are, they are not always effective at resolving differing points of view in a reasonable time. A live discussion can greatly accelerate such conversations.

The second reason to hold a review meeting is to encourage participation. This participation occurs partly as a function of scheduling the meeting. Assuming you set expectations that everyone should arrive to the meeting well prepared, this will encourage reviewers who haven't yet read the design to do so. It is also your opportunity to solicit input from everyone who, whether they have read the design or not, has not yet commented or otherwise contributed.

Meetings can be used to encourage a diversity of thought, which is highly desirable, although these contributions must be handled carefully. Without strong moderation, meetings can be readily dominated by those most comfortable speaking up in front of others and quickest with their thoughts. Moderators can counter this by actively soliciting feedback from all participants, one by one. Note that the written design documentation and asynchronous review that have happened prior to this point will have given every participant everything they need to be prepared when they are asked for their input.

When conducting review meetings, pay attention to the meeting dynamic. Review meetings should not be overly contentious; the debate must be about the design, not the people. At the same time, the goal of a review is not to build rapport. In fact, a meeting in which everyone is getting along too well can reduce the chances of someone raising a countervailing point of view. Good team rapport is valuable; building it will require investment outside of review meetings.

Status

As a team can have many change proposals in flight at once, everyone will benefit from good bookkeeping. I recommend keeping all change proposals for the project in one place. Separate those that are in progress from the completed ones. You want the in-progress items, which form a smaller set, to be easily accessible so that everyone can find them quickly. Completed proposals should be kept for reference but moved out of the way—perhaps into a separate folder. Over time you'll collect many completed proposals; sorting them by date can help keep things organized.

Be sure to note and maintain the status of each document within the document itself, and a status field should be part of your proposal template. At a minimum, you'll need to track four values: in progress, under review, approved, and rejected. You may find it valuable to use more values to track more nuanced states. For example, some teams use an "on hold" status for proposals that have been set aside, but to which they expect to return.

The review process described in the previous section applies to proposals in the middle state: under review. Although I encourage everyone to work in the open, the "in progress" status signals that the author is not yet ready for the review process to begin. The design may be incomplete, or still undergoing radical changes—either way, a reviewer could be wasting their time.

It's just as important to let participants know that once a document is approved, it can no longer be reviewed. This rule will bother people who would like to make further changes, whether to add new features or correct mistakes, real or perceived, in the approved proposals. Remind them that the process is iterative, and the way to make further changes is via a new change proposal.

Your review process should also establish, for each review, the participants and their roles. Clearly, each review has an author, who is responsible for the design. You will also need to designate, at a minimum, reviewers and approvers.

In the spirit of working in the open, I recommend making the reviewer role open, in the sense that anyone can participate. Occasionally someone will abuse this privilege, but firm adherence to the review process will limit that impact. Nonetheless, you may be aware of someone who really ought to review a given design—perhaps because of their experience or familiarity with the topic—and you'll need to make an explicit assignment.

Most of your attention, though, should go into selecting approvers. Approvers are the people who must sign off on a design before it's done. Unlike with reviewers, the author cannot simply "agree to disagree" when the approvers' opinions differ from the author's—at least not unless the approvers are also satisfied with the outcome.

Your list of approvers should contain individuals who bear accountability for making the change successful. For example, I'm often an approver on changes authored by someone on my team—especially if those changes make significant revisions to the architecture of the system. By taking accountability and signing off on the change,

I'm not only approving the changes, but also committing my energy to seeing them through to a successful outcome.

It's critical that approvers realize that, by approving a change, they are committing themselves to the outcome. People often misunderstand this role and take approval to be either purely an assessment of the change ("good enough") or simply an exercise in process ("checking boxes"). You can tell that this has happened when problems arise later and your approvers assert that they never liked the change, never agreed with it, or—worst of all—hadn't read it. That's a bad outcome for you, for them, and for the project.

A good set of approvers, then, consists of three to four people with a stake in its realization. Who those people are will necessarily depend on the structure of your organization. At a minimum, it should include someone who has responsibility for the implementation; that can be an engineer or an architect. And, as noted earlier, architectural leaders also have a stake in these changes.

For all these same reasons, I don't recommend more than four approvers. Beyond that number, accountability—that commitment to seeing the change through—is diluted. Approvers tend to focus on "their piece" instead of the whole change, to everyone's detriment. If the implementation effort involves a large team, it's the commitment of one or two leaders that we're looking for here.

You may find that this model puts pressure on your engineering and architecture leaders, as they'll be asked to approve a substantial number of changes. Leaders can and should delegate reviews to members of their team. Delegation not only helps them manage their workload but also gets the team—which clearly has a stake in the outcome—involved.

Velocity

Product organizations are governed by schedules and budgets. Architecture teams should support these goals by conducting their work in a predictable fashion. Resist the urge to look at schedules, budgets, and people as arbitrary constraints.

These considerations should, instead, be part of your process. Your team's goal in developing a new service should not be to find the "best" architecture—a label that is ultimately meaningless without defined criteria. It should be to find an architecture that meets the requirements and that the team can build given the project parameters. Architecture costs, implementation costs, and operational costs should all be considered during the design process.

The estimation process can be overdone, mostly by trying to achieve unreasonable specificity. When starting a change, it helps to know whether it will take a few days or a few months to complete. It's important to know whether a change will take a month or a year to implement. But as these are merely estimates, differences between 30 days and 31 days are meaningless.

The rough estimates need not take much time to develop, and data gathered on prior work is helpful here. The time spent on a change proposal in the motivational and conceptual stages varies wildly, making these timelines less useful to track. Instead, focus on recording when the detailed design process gets under way, when reviews start, and when approval is reached. If you see large ranges, try bucketing the changes into three or so categories based on the rough size of the change.

When you're starting a new change, work from this set of data instead of trying to make an uninformed prediction. Which previous changes were like this one, and were they small, medium, or large in scope? What's the range of times those changes have taken in the past? If you've been collecting data along the way, that exercise needn't take more than about five minutes.

It can be helpful to think in ranges, and I recommend this as a general practice for estimates, whether the issue at hand is time frames or dollars. For example, perhaps your data shows that "medium" changes take 4 to 6 weeks to complete. Better, then, to estimate the next similarly sized design as needing 4 to 6 weeks of work, not 5 weeks. When people are given just one number, it anchors their expectations around that one point. That's fine for a measurement, but it's not how estimates work. By providing estimates as ranges—two numbers—listeners are forced to think about the uncertainty, and the amount of uncertainty is conveyed by the size of the range.

Every team will work at a different pace and structure their work in a different way. Thus, it's impossible to provide anything like a comprehensive sense of "typical" times; I can only speak to the projects that I've worked on.

With that caveat, while running the architecture for one project, we kept detailed records on the time it took to complete the detailed design stage of each change proposal. A "typical" design could be completed in 4 to 6 weeks. Using that data, I could both set expectations for new designs and easily compute the teams' throughput. (Each architect generally had two designs in progress at any given time.)

The really fascinating thing about making schedules and budgets part of the process, though, is that it creates a feedback loop. For example, after my team measured our design time and established 4 to 6 weeks as typical, our detailed design stage became *more* predictable. I believe a couple of factors drove this effect.

First, simply knowing the range sets expectations. That is, when starting a new detailed design, the author can't ignore the expected timeline, or imagine that they have months to complete the work. The task at hand is no longer "complete this detailed design"; instead, it's "complete this detailed design within what we all know to be the expected time frame." Establishing a range focuses the mind.

Second, a clear definition of "typical" makes variations from the norm more obvious. Suppose that at week four of the detailed design work, it's clear that work won't be finished anytime soon. Instead of trundling along, we have a clear indicator that something is off. There can be any number of reasons for this: higher-priority interruptions, too large a piece of work, unsettled requirements. The point isn't that we know what's gone wrong but that a red flag indicates something is off, giving us an impetus to chase it down.

At all costs, avoid the trap of setting up an architecture in opposition to reasonable schedules. If your conceptual approach will take three months of detailed design but you have only one month available, look for another approach. That isn't always possible, but a more expensive approach requires strong justification. There's nothing effective about an architecture practice that chooses the slower, more expensive approach.

Thinking

Product development is a team effort, so we spend a good deal of time on coordination (via tools and processes) and communication (written and verbal). Yet, in the end, the real work happens via individual contributions derived from our ability to think it through. And thinking takes time.

Architecture is, by its very nature, about the coordination of different system components. In consequence, most architects will find themselves with no shortage of documents to write, documents to review, and conversations to hold. These demands on our time are not unique to architecture. The point here is that there's a bias in the system: It's easy to see that we must spend time on these activities. However, it seems harder to recognize and set aside time to focus on thinking—despite that being the activity at the core of the discipline.

When we think about our personal schedules and managing our calendars, we tend to focus on using them as tools for coordination with others. Who hasn't experienced the joy of scheduling a meeting with a dozen participants across four time zones? Many calendaring programs are chock-full of features designed to make this easier—which lures us into thinking that's what time management is about.

To be an effective and productive architect, however, requires setting aside time to think. But note that, despite the need to write things down, jumping straight to writing can be a hindrance. You'll find writing easier once your thinking has crystallized, and you'll find thinking more difficult when you're slowing it down by trying to type it in as you go. If your writing isn't flowing, your best option might be to step away from the keyboard.

Your team can use their calendars to create time for thinking, just as you can use it to set aside time for meetings. Encourage—even require—that everyone block out thinking time; label it "focus time" or the like. (Your team may have to agree to a common time to make this work.) I strive to keep focus time on my work calendar every day. If my day was full of meetings, how would I be getting any work done at all?

If you find your workdays filling up with meetings, prioritize. Using a time management matrix [9] or equivalent tool, assess whether each item is important (or unimportant) and urgent (or not urgent).

If it's not important, don't do it! That sounds obvious but can be difficult to put into practice. After all, sometimes unimportant things are fun, or interesting, or distracting. To test if something is unimportant, I like to ask myself: If I ignored this, what would happen? If the answer is "nothing bad," then ignoring it is my best option.

You should strive to keep important and urgent work to a minimum. When you're working in this zone, you're under the most pressure and it is, therefore, where the most mistakes are made. Items in this category will never go to zero because they are often exogenous in nature; it may be impossible to see them coming. Still, the less often they pop up, the better you'll be able to deal with them.

To the extent that you can avoid important and urgent work, it's done by setting aside sufficient time for important but not urgent work. In this zone, you're getting out ahead of crises before they happen. I like to think of this work as preparing a plan and filing it away for later. When the urgent request comes in, I simply reach into my (virtual) filing cabinet to find a plan, ready to go.

I don't want to minimize how difficult this is to achieve, as many organizations operate primarily in the important/urgent quadrant. At the same time, architecture has a specific responsibility to think about the future and anticipate what will become urgent but has not yet done so. It's right up front in the definition of architecture: *principles governing its design and evolution.* What are principles for evolution if not thinking in advance?

Summary

Software design work cannot be completed at the same steady, predictable rate in the way that manufactured products might exit an assembly line in a factory. Nonetheless, an effective software architecture team adheres to a set of practices that support an organization's broader goals of delivering the right product at the right time.

These practices start with an architectural backlog, which captures all the changes that a team has considered, completed, and rejected, and contemplates doing in the future, as a catalog of change proposals. The backlog tracks current work, helping to keep designs and reviews on track. It is a reliable memory of potential future work as well, helping teams set such items aside for later. And it provides data for managing team velocity.

Catalogs of software components and data models help document the current system and thus accelerate design. Templates further accelerate design work by making it easier to author new and complete designs, and by simplifying the review process.

Review is an essential part of the design process. A review process should encompass both asynchronous and synchronous modes, supported by appropriate tools and processes. Track and make visible the status of each design and the role of each review participant to keep the review running smoothly.

By managing these practices well—and setting aside time for the thinking required to both design and review—software teams can scope and estimate their work. Using these abilities, they can be strong partners with engineering and others.

Chapter 8
Communication

An architecture practice exists to define and evolve the architecture of the system it oversees. Over the last few chapters, we've discussed how to manage a system's evolution via a change process that starts from a motivation, moves on to a conceptual approach, and then produces a detailed design. Along the way, we've described how visions, standards, principles, catalogs, dictionaries, and more help support these practices. In short, an architecture practice produces a lot of information.

But how do you get that information into the hands of your colleagues, partners, and others? Not all of it should go to everyone, of course—we want to get the right information to the right people. While we're at it, we should get the timing right, too. We should push important updates to them and let them discover other information on demand. It's a lot to manage. Closing that gap requires communication, and an effective software architecture practice requires effective communication practices.

Written documentation lays the groundwork for effective communication. Writing things down forces a clarity of thought that's often lacking in conversations and presentations, on the part of both the author and the reader. It can be consumed at any time and any pace. Best of all, it is a scalable investment, as easily read by a thousand people as by a hundred.

However, communication involves more than writing. As architects, the communication we strive for results in shared understanding, and understanding requires conversation. In a conversation, information flows in both directions, and the conversing parties use that flow to identify and close gaps in their common understanding.

At the same time, more is not always better—too much communication can also get in the way of understanding. That happens when information isn't organized or discoverable, when terminology isn't used consistently, or when current and accurate information can't be distinguished from old and outdated information. Countering these tendencies through information architecture, naming, and other practices will further support communication and understanding.

Ultimately, it's feedback from other people that will confirm whether your communication efforts are effective. If they're not, you can iteratively refine them in much the same way as your software designs. Every person and every team have their own preferred modes of communication; you'll be better off finding what works for your team than following rigid guidelines.

Mental Models

When people internalize knowledge about a system, they construct a mental model based on their understanding of the concepts embodied in that system, and they use this model to reason about the system. Mental models are intrinsic to how people understand the world around them and are not unique to software.

In *The Design of Everyday Things* [10], Don Norman shares an anecdote regarding his mental model of his refrigerator. The refrigerator has two compartments: a refrigerator section that keeps food cold but not frozen, and a freezer section that keeps its contents frozen. Each section has a separate temperature control.

In Norman's mental model of his refrigerator, the two sections operated independently. That model is suggested by the controls, which do not suggest any connection between the two. When the food in his freezer was too cold, he turned the freezer temperature up. He didn't expect that this adjustment to the freezer would make the refrigerator section colder.

Unfortunately, his mental model did not correspond to the refrigerator's operational concepts. The refrigerator only measured the temperature in the refrigerator section. What appeared to be a separate control for the freezer operated by shifting the relative cooling of the two sections. Thus, making the freezer warmer would always make the refrigerator colder—unless the refrigerator setting was also adjusted.

The core concept in the refrigerator's design was a single cooling source that could be shared unequally between the two compartments. Once you know it's a single source, it's straightforward to reason that an adjustment—to either the source or the sharing—necessarily affects both compartments.

Fortunately for Norman, he had a working refrigerator with which to experiment. He first adjusted the controls according to his mental model of the refrigerator's operation. When that didn't work, he understood that his mental model didn't match the refrigerator's conceptual model. After some trial and error, he was able to determine how the appliance worked—and updated his understanding accordingly.

When designing software, we rely on our communication skills to capture and convey the conceptual models that animate our systems. Unlike Norman, who had to accept his refrigerator for what it was, architects often do this in advance of building a specific product or capability. That makes us much more dependent on our ability to cultivate shared understanding through communication, rather than experimentation.

Indeed, the best test of whether communication has delivered understanding occurs when someone else uses their mental model (i.e., their understanding) to describe the system's conceptual model back to you. If that conceptual model matches what you first described to them, the model has survived the round trip, and you have a shared understanding. It's not shared in the sense that the other person has memorized a diagram or a list of design principles; memorization does not imply understanding. What we're looking for here is internalization and understanding sufficient to re-articulate the same information in equivalent form.

Thus, a system's architecture embodies many concepts, and everyone—its designers, its builders, and its users—construct mental models based on their understanding of those concepts. When those concepts are clearly communicated, their mental models will be aligned. Everyone will then have a shared and correct understanding of how the system works.

In my experience, nothing more strongly correlates with a product team's ability to deliver with quality and velocity than a shared understanding of the system concepts. Of course, this doesn't guarantee commercial success, which is impacted by many other variables. Rather, when teams are strongly aligned, they will function efficiently and effectively in moving toward a common goal. They avoid pulling in different directions, taking too long to make decisions, and heading down dead ends. Those behaviors all result from a lack of understanding.

How do teams develop this common understanding? Through sustained, ongoing communication. Only when there's back-and-forth dialogue can we test and verify our shared understanding. Achieving a shared mental model is the goal of an architect's communication efforts.

Writing

There's more to communication than documentation, but documentation remains an essential element of communication. For a variety of reasons, I recommend that teams establish writing as the default form of communication and layer on presentations and conversations.

This recommendation arises in part from the simple observation that it is increasingly less common for members of a team to all be in one place—or even in one time zone. Even before the COVID-19 pandemic, distributed teams were becoming increasingly common. That trend is partly driven by companies opening multiple offices and partly attributable to employees who work from home.

In fact, while some corporations have spent years and a good deal of money striving to bring their employees together in one location, successful counterexamples abound. Open-source projects, for example, typically don't have the luxury of gathering contributors: The contributors are self-selected, they live where they live, and the project probably doesn't have a travel budget.

In fact, for many years, open-source projects have been using "asynchronous" communication, which essentially comes down to various forms of written communication. Whether it's email, chat, an issue tracker, code reviews, a wiki, or, more likely, some combination of these—all are forms of written communication.

As the "asynchronous" label indicates, this approach has the advantage that it doesn't require people to come together at a designated time and place to communicate. In the extreme, that might be impractical: There aren't many hours during the day that are convenient for two individuals who live in time zones more than eight hours apart. But even colleagues in the same time zone can appreciate the chance to defer an interruption until later. Many people find it helpful to create uninterrupted blocks of time to get meaningful work done.

Asynchronous communication is also difficult, insofar as the participants won't have the same mental state when writing versus reading. That's quite different from a live conversation, where the shared state built up over the duration of the conversation can lead to quick yet meaningful exchanges.

For any nontrivial exchange, use a tool with collaboration capabilities. If the document is prose, then a wiki will work well. If the document is code, then use a code review system. Any tool that supports inline, threaded comments will do the trick.

Try to avoid email and chat for anything substantial. As communication tools, they have a couple of drawbacks. First, both email and chat encourage brief messages and responses. And if they're too brief, they tend to devolve into long, confused exchanges that are trying to clarify the original question, understand the answer, or both. Even worse, it's difficult to connect the responses with the original text—exactly the problem that inline comments solve in a good collaboration tool.

Sometimes, though, you might work with someone who takes the time to write long, detailed emails that do a wonderful job of explaining the issue at hand. Now the content is great, but the audience is wrong because the email was, inevitably, sent to only some subset of the people who need this information. Of course, it can be forwarded, and maybe found again later, but these are terrible ways to manage important information.

As a rule of thumb, if you find yourself writing one of these emails—or receiving one—turn it into a document and send a link instead. Where you record the document is critical but, if you do this properly, it will be easily found again later. (More on this in the "Information Architecture" section.) Anyone who clicks on the link will be taken to the current version of the document, rather than whichever version was frozen in time in the original email. And, best of all, they can participate in the conversation by commenting on the document itself, for all to see.

These practical and logistical arguments have all been cited in support of writing documents: This practice respects where people live and when they work, it leads to better exchanges, and it helps make important information accessible. But there's another reason to favor written communication: Writing is hard.

It might seem paradoxical to recommend something hard as your preferred communication method, but writing is hard for a reason: To write clearly about something, we must understand it well; to understand it well, we must think it through. And thinking it through is precisely what we want to encourage architects to do.

Note that I am not suggesting that everyone ought to think things through and "get it right" before they write their ideas down and share them. That would replace communication with isolation, which is the opposite of what we're trying to achieve. But we also don't want to waste anyone's time with communication that doesn't make sense. Readers might disagree with what's written, but to do that, they still need to understand it. What we're demanding here is clarity, not correctness.

In fact, anyone who thinks they've gotten it right the first time is probably wrong, anyway. In the spirit of creating a dialogue, the author's job is to write up a clear description of their best understanding of the issue or design at that moment—and they are doing so to seek feedback. They are seeking feedback because their understanding is insufficient in some way that they cannot yet see. A useful dialogue begins with a clear description and elicits a clear response. That is the essence of working in the open.

Written documentation is also the most scalable form of communication in existence. That's why the printing press was revolutionary. Books existed before the press, but the press lowered the cost of their duplication and thus increased their dissemination. Computers have driven those costs to effectively zero, so once you've written a document, there's really nothing to prevent its distribution to as many people as necessary.

With great power comes great responsibility. Share a well-written document that communicates with clarity, and your ability to share that document broadly can advance your project, build a better product, and ship it sooner. But distribute a poorly written document that confuses everyone who reads it, and you've done nothing more than waste a lot of people's time and energy.

Talking

While written communication is essential, some situations call for a live conversation. Conversations are especially helpful when a team does not yet have a shared understanding of a system's concepts. Once the team has defined those concepts, they provide common ground for follow-on work, including even changes to the concepts itself. However, until that happens, bootstrapping into that first common conversation can be difficult.

Conversations don't seem to be essential, even at the bootstrapping stage. For example, sometimes an individual with a clear concept and a great write-up will get the whole thing started. In fact, sometimes entire projects get started this way: The individual vision comes first, followed by a written proposal, and then the team is built around it.

More often, though, teams are brought together around a new challenge, so the first step is entirely about developing concepts as a starting point. At this stage, the concepts don't have to be correct, or complete, or even very extensive to serve their purpose. Their initial purpose is as much about aligning on a common understanding of the problem as it is about aligning on a conceptual approach.

In these situations—that is, when teams are newly formed—conversations have an important secondary benefit in building team rapport. Individuals who don't know, trust, and respect each other aren't a team—they're just a group of people. Turning a group into a team takes time and can't be rushed, but it will happen faster through live conversation than via emails and messages.

Conversations don't need to be held in person and, for some teams, that's not an option. However, there is value in bringing everyone physically together, both when forming a new team and on an ongoing basis. Chapter 9 discusses these and other aspects of the architecture team at more length.

The value in live conversation does not end, of course, after these initial talks. Sometimes a discussion simply won't settle down, no matter how many written proposals and asynchronous reviews have taken place. It's not reasonable to let that discourse go on forever, especially if deadlines loom.

That's okay; schedule a conversation to resolve it. Here the investment in the written documentation and asynchronous reviews will pay off because when the meeting starts everyone already has a detailed understanding of the issue at hand. These meetings aren't about establishing concepts; they're about resolving differing points of view based on those concepts. An hour will often suffice for such meetings, and limiting the time available can help everyone focus.

So far, we've discussed topic-driven conversations. That is, these conversations have been either prompted by a larger need, such as bootstrapping a new project, or scheduled to discuss an issue that merits conversation. These conversations benefit from standard advice regarding good meetings: establishing clear topics, providing an agenda, and so on.

Another kind of conversational space inverts this model. Instead of being driven by a topic, it's driven by the calendar. This engagement occurs regularly, perhaps once a week. And it's long enough to have a meaningful conversation—an hour at a minimum—but not so long as to be burdensome, given its cadence.

With the right cadence, this approach creates a space for the team to have an ongoing conversation. The gaps between these dialogues must be small enough that the conversation can be easily restarted; that is, everyone must remember where it was left off last time. And the duration must be long enough that progress can be made in the time allotted.

These long-running conversations serve two purposes. First, they tend to surface topics that are not urgent enough to demand their own meetings yet are important enough to merit attention. Such topics cannot always be dispatched on the spot. Often, they must be added to the backlog to be revisited later. Alternatively, they may become agenda items for a topic-driven meeting, where more time can be allotted.

These long-running conversations also complement less frequent in-person gatherings by creating a space in which the conversation can move forward between get-togethers. This is where the use of a regular cadence is critical: Because everyone has set aside the time for these conversations, it's okay to discuss topics that might not reach resolution for weeks or months. It's actually the opposite of the "every meeting needs an agenda and decisions" approach that's supposed to make for a productive meeting, but that's the point: Conversations need time and space.

If, for any reason, you're not able to bring your team together physically—say, during a pandemic—then consider creating or bolstering a conversational forum in its place. Meet a bit more frequently or make the meetings a bit longer. It might be a poor substitute for meeting in person but it's far better than choking off the conversation.

No matter how you structure your conversations, no decision should be considered final until it's captured, reviewed, and agreed to in written form. It's tempting to skip this step because it seemed so clear in the moment that everyone was finally aligned—but skipping this step is always a mistake.

First, what seemed like alignment during the conversation might not have been after all. Maybe someone misunderstood what they were agreeing to. Maybe someone has second thoughts. Maybe someone objected at the time but didn't feel comfortable speaking up. Take the time to prepare and distribute a written version of the decision. If these issues apply, they'll be raised then—and you can address them earlier rather than later. If no objections crop up at this point, then you can move forward with more confidence.

Second, whatever you decided will inevitably impact more people than those who participated in the conversation. Maybe someone couldn't attend. Maybe the attendees were a subset of a large team—not everyone can be in every meeting. Or maybe your new hire is starting next week and will want to catch up on this decision. A written record makes the decision durable and accessible.

Talking has its place. It's essential to building team rapport and sometimes the best option for accelerating progress on tough issues. But it is a complement to—not a substitute for—writing things down.

Information Architecture

When there's an emphasis on written communication, architects on a sizable project soon find themselves managing a large set of artifacts: proposals, specifications, standards, and more. Often, architects also prepare presentations, newsletters, blog entries, and other less-formal artifacts that also aid communication.

It is important to invest time in managing these materials. Absent curation, you will inevitably end up with a disorganized mess. People will find it difficult to find the documentation they need. Some will attempt to cope with this chaos by asking around until they find what they're looking for; while a reasonable response on their part, that's taxing for everyone.

Others will conclude that what they're looking for doesn't exist. Lack of information will then hamper their future designs. In the best-case scenario, this gap in their information base is caught by a knowledgeable reviewer before the work is done. In the worst case, duplicate functionality may be built because its creator simply didn't know that the system already had what they needed.

Similar failures readily occur with standards. If a standard has been created but can't be found, what good can come of it? Failure to adhere to an important standard is doubly wasteful because the failure is often identified only after some work has been done on a nonstandard approach. Standards should accelerate design and development, but that happens only if they're used from the get-go.

To make the most of the artifacts produced—and to avoid the failures that occur when those artifacts are not well organized—teams must maintain an *information architecture*. Information architecture is the discipline of organizing information to facilitate its use. In other words, it specifies how and where you store these artifacts so that they can be found and used.

To set up an information architecture, it helps to begin with a categorization of the documents your team produces. Here are some categories commonly used for this purpose:

- **Backlog entries:** These records contain the project's "to-do list" of architectural work, as discussed in Chapters 4 and 7.
- **Specifications:** These are the authoritative descriptions for each system element—libraries, services, applications, subsystems, and so on.
- **Change proposals:** Each change proposal describes a proposed set of additions, deletions, and changes to the system's architecture or designs. Its status, authors, and approvers should be prominently displayed.
- **Standards:** These documents describe the set of standards to which all architecture and design work must adhere. They include the architectural principles to which that work conforms.
- **Guides:** A guide provides a conceptual description of a system component. It complements the specifications, which are highly technical, with a more accessible explanation.

- **Vision papers:** Vision papers articulate the desired state of a system or subsystem in a three- to five-year time frame. (See Chapter 4 for more on vision papers.)
- **Presentations:** Presentations are records of live explanations or discussions of a system, or some part thereof. Keep the slide deck and, if possible, a recording of the presentation.
- **Catalogs and dictionaries:** As explained in Chapter 7, catalogs document a system's software elements and data models. Dictionaries, discussed later in this chapter, define a system's terminology.
- **Notes:** Notes are a catch-all, handy for documenting an argument or point of view that isn't ready to fit into any other category as, say, a change proposal or presentation.
- **Blog entries:** If you have a large audience who appreciate regular updates, find a medium for publishing those. Blogs can work well; email newsletters and the like also work.

These artifacts should be organized in a taxonomy that will help everyone find the right item at the right time. The team should maintain this on some well-known web page. However, you don't need to, and probably don't want to, store all these items in a single tool. Perhaps there's a single tool that can handle backlogs, change proposals, specifications, blog entries, and other items well—but I've never found it. As a rule of thumb, the greater the breadth of a tool, the more it compromises its abilities in any given area. Fortunately, every tool supports links, so different tools can be woven together in a single taxonomy.

Here's a basic taxonomy that will work for most projects:

- **Publications:** Finished documents that describe your system appear first, under publications. Within that category, materials are generally organized from the broadest audience to the narrowest.

  - Blog entries
  - Guides
  - Papers
  - Specifications

- Standards
- Notes

- **Work in progress:** Next comes work in progress, which organizes the project's proposals. Note that they are further subdivided by status. "Inactive" proposals are those that haven't been approved, but they're not done either—they're on hold, possibly with the intention to take them up again later. If you're sure you won't return to something, however, you can discard it instead.

  - Active proposals
  - Approved proposals
  - Inactive proposals

- **References:** Catalogs and dictionaries fall later on the list. This is also a good place to curate lists of other resources, such as corporate or industry references. The materials here will often be referenced directly (i.e., via links to catalog or dictionary entries) from other documents as well.

  - Software catalog
  - Data model catalog
  - Dictionary

- **Planning:** Here is where the team can store the material most relevant for internal use, such as the backlog. In the spirit of working in the open, this material should be made available along with everything else. Most readers won't be looking for it, so it's appropriate to place it last on the list.

  - Backlog
  - Team information

Even though proposals are central to an architect's day-to-day work, organize your taxonomy to de-emphasize them. Guides, papers, specifications—these all go first because they're what your most casual readers are looking for, and these people won't have the patience to dig around for the desired materials. Proposals should be further organized into active, approved, and inactive.

Accurate labeling of each artifact is critical. Start with a status, which should be prominently displayed for each. Is it a draft? Under review? Current? Outdated? Status is critical information for your readers. They don't want to spend their time reading outdated documentation, acting too early on a change proposal that hasn't yet been approved, and so on.

Version Confusion

Once, when starting a new project, I was handed a large set of specifications for the system. As I read through them, I became increasingly confused. Some of the subsystems made sense on their own, but many seemed duplicative, and I couldn't understand how they fit together. It felt as if the more I read, the less I understood. It would be another month before someone explained to me that I had been handed documentation for both a "version 1" system and a rewritten "version 2," which had nothing in common with the former. Unfortunately for me, no one had bothered to label the documents according to which version of the system they documented.

Remember that organizing all these materials is the beginning of the job, not the end. Updating these documents should be part of the checklist accompanying each item. Was a proposal approved? Move it from Active Proposals to Approved Proposals. Did you adopt a new standard? Make sure it's published (or linked) from Publications/Standards. And so on.

If interested parties can subscribe to notifications when new items are uploaded or linked, let them know how to take advantage of that feature. I also recommend writing a blog post (or equivalent) each time a proposal is approved, a new specification is created, or other major changes occur. Consider making a blog entry part of your approval checklist.

These blog posts don't have to be long, because their purpose is simply to make readers aware of the change. Anyone who wants to know the details can, after all, go read the specification, standard, or other document that the post references. Your readers will appreciate it, though: A paragraph or two can be more informative than what they're likely to get out of any built-in notification mechanism.

If you can, collect statistics on the use of these materials. There's enormous value in comprehensive, accurate, written documentation: It needs to be written only once, but there's no limit on the number of people who can read it. You might be surprised at how frequently some documents are consulted.

Conversely, if you don't see much traffic to these documents, it merits some investigation. Can readers find them, or do you have a discoverability issue? Are the documents useful, or are readers turned away because what they're reading is full of jargon, outdated, or something else?

Information, like code, rots if left unattended. Set aside some time to periodically review your documentation. Are the documents in the right places? Marked with the correct status? If there's a significant gap, consider adding a backlog item to address it. If necessary, move outdated documents to an archive, where they can be maintained without cluttering up day-to-day discovery.

Naming Things

As teams develop concepts, they'll find themselves coining lots of names. Concepts themselves need names, and often involve many constituent components that do, too. Teams also need names for layers, patterns, components, entities, properties, classes, variables, messages, schemas, and more. You'll also need to name the artifacts, processes, and tools that aren't the system itself but are essential to its creation and maintenance. Any reasonably complex system will require names for hundreds of items, and those items will range from simple, discrete concepts to terms that encompass tens or hundreds of concepts wrapped into a single system component.

Invest in good names; good names unlock every other aspect of communication. They facilitate the development and understanding of conceptual models. They're essential to written documentation, which is often consumed by a reader who cannot immediately ask for clarification of new or confusing names. And they reduce the chances that participants in a conversation will speak past each other. Effort spent on coming up with good names will pay off.

First and foremost, good names are descriptive. Did you create a service that converts entities from one format to another? "Babel" is a clever name, and some might catch the allusion. But "Entity Format Conversion Service" is a better name because it tells the reader what the service does. It avoids creating a burden on the reader to remember, infer, or look up its behavior each time the name is encountered.

Similarly, you should never use code names unless secrecy is required. Remember that code names are designed to hide and obfuscate. It might sound cool to call your work "Project X"—but the inevitable result is that no one will know what you're talking about. That's great if you're trying to keep it a secret but terrible for furthering communication.

Avoid merely clever names, too. I once worked on a project that had a data migration tool called "Mayfly." The general idea was that the tool was going to live for only a day, as mayflies live for just one day (or two) in their adult form. Of course, the tool lived longer, the name no longer made sense, and there was no obvious connection to its function. Engineers on that team spent years answering questions about that name.

For the same reasons, acronyms should be used sparingly. They can be helpful when dealing with long names, although it's better to just find a short name. And they work best when they are not words, as that weakens the association with their actual meaning. Call your Translation for Entities Service "TEsS"—a not uncommon woman's name in some places—and you risk your listeners wondering if you're speaking of software or a new teammate's multilingual abilities. (They may also find the inconsistent capitalization irritating.)

As most systems require many names, they should also follow a consistent structure. Doing so further reduces the cognitive load associated with each label. When organized correctly, the structure reflects actual relationships between different concepts. Use of the terms and structure thus creates a secondary communication channel, providing additional information via implication without requiring explicit restatement.

For example, suppose you are working on a commerce system. You'll have to store two addresses for each sale: one for billing and one for shipping. You could call the first one Billing Address and the second one Shipping Location, but that is a poor choice because it hides the implicit connection: Both are addresses. It's also troublesome when you want to refer to both at once. Collectively, are they an address? A location? An "address and a location"?

Better to adopt a structure: Billing Address, Shipping Address, Address. These names are not exciting or clever, but they are descriptive and rich. They are individually and collectively self-explanatory.

The structure that's used in this example is straightforward and powerful. There's a simple name for the core concept—Address, in this case. Related concepts are named by adding adjectives as qualifiers: Billing and Shipping. This naming structure is quite common, if not commonly remarked upon.

One can easily extend this structure. For example, is a customer updating their Billing Address? Then they're replacing their *Old Billing Address* with their *New Billing Address*. You can always prefix yet another adjective to disambiguate these concepts.

One can also tack on additional nouns as a suffix. Are Addresses stored in a discrete service? Then you may find it useful to note that Address Entities are stored in the Address Service, and they're updated via an Address Update. How all this works should be described in the Address Service Specification. You will find yourself spending less time explaining how concepts relate when the connection is obvious and easy to remember based on their names.

Consistency should be extended more broadly when feasible. For example, many systems record some basic metadata for each entity: when it was created, when it was last updated, and so on. These properties should have the same names everywhere they appear. They should adopt the same form as well: "created" and "modified" are a good pair; "createDate" and "modificationTime" are not. A lot of time and trouble can be saved, both when defining names and when using them, by picking a form and sticking with it. Even more time can be saved if you can adopt a form from a relevant standard, avoiding the need for your team to align on their own rules.

Should you need to change a name, do so comprehensively. It's better to change a name than to continue using one that's misleading. Continuing to use both the old and new names is even worse. Therefore, when names do change, it's critical to apply that change to existing specifications, standards, and other impacted documentation.

Name changes are a good example of the "change proposals as patches" metaphor. The change proposal will use both names, old and new, as well as explain why the change is being made; it's the link between the two terms. Once approved, that change proposal "patch" is applied to every document that uses the old term. (Old change proposals, however, should not be updated.) A name change has been handled well when a new member of the team can work without knowing that the old name was once in use.

Finally, when you change names, it is important to hold people accountable for using the new names in conversation as well as in writing. It can be uncomfortable to correct people—or be corrected—as the switchover occurs and the old name is used out of habit. Nonetheless, corrections will probably be necessary to cement use of the new name, as otherwise mentions of the old term will be taken as tacit approval for its continued use.

Dictionaries

Consistent, descriptive names are all well and good and should be backed by clear and concise definitions. Writing a definition for each term serves two purposes. First, it serves as an authority should ambiguity or misunderstanding arise. Second, and more importantly, it forces conceptual clarity. More than once I've seen teams struggle to write a definition for a term that they thought they already understood.

Dictionaries work best when they are woven into the fabric of your documentation. Wherever you maintain your system, each definition should have a unique URL to which other documents can link. For example, individual wiki pages work well; rows in a spreadsheet do not. If you can, use one of the same tools you use for change proposals, specifications, or other artifacts.

Each document should link to the dictionary for each first use of a word. Linking subsequent uses of the term in the same document is tedious and unnecessary. It makes more work for the author, without adding any value. And because links are made visually distinct via typographic differences of one kind or another, too many links are tiresome for the reader as well.

Although common in many specification templates, documents should generally not contain their own "Terminology" sections. If they do, they're either duplicating the dictionary entry (and better served by a link) or using a different definition, which creates confusion. Exceptions should be made only when a document uses terminology that falls outside the scope of the system dictionary and when a proposal introduces new terminology.

Speaking of scope, avoid redefining terms with standard definitions. If industry-standard definitions are available, link to those instead. Doing so saves you the time and trouble of reproducing those definitions, and it reinforces the link to those standards. In addition, it helps new participants leverage their industry knowledge when learning about your system.

As an author, if you find yourself trying to link to a dictionary entry that isn't present, stop and create an entry for it. Applying some discipline on this point may feel painful at first. However, once a good set of definitions has been built up, you won't encounter this situation as frequently. And there's no better metric for what a dictionary should contain than the set of definitions required by the system's documentation.

Change proposals are necessarily an exception to this rule. Remember that when you're writing a change proposal, you're proposing something new, and it doesn't become part of the system until the change has been approved. If the change involves defining new terminology, then those entries must not be added to the dictionary before the change is approved. Change proposals should, therefore, include their own definitions for all new terminology. After they're approved, those definitions move into the dictionary, which then becomes the authoritative source.

As your project dictionary grows, some organization is in order. I recommend creating a classification system and tagging each entry accordingly. For example, you might tag entries based on their relationship to systems, domains, layers, services, or data models. When picking a tool for maintaining your dictionary, look for the ability to tag and generate lists by tag in addition to unique URLs for each entry.

Dictionary entries are documents—albeit small ones—and should have their own template. I recommend using these sections:

- **Excerpt:** Start with a one-sentence definition that can be used as an excerpt in another context.
- **Detail:** Additional text that rounds out the excerpt.
- **See also:** Related terms or lists of terms.
- **References:** Links to specifications or other documentation directly related to this term.

Finally, be sure to link to other terms that appear in these definitions. That tends to happen a lot; two or three links in the excerpt alone is not uncommon. It may take some time to build up these definitions and links. However, once they're established, you may be amazed to find how much you can learn about a system just by navigating through its dictionary.

Listening

Just as we don't know if a product has hit the mark until customers respond, we don't know if our communication efforts are effective until we've heard from the people with whom we're communicating. We can write for them, talk to them, and organize, name, and define the things we're writing about and talking about. But until our counterparts understand what we're communicating, we're still short of our mark.

To know if we've been understood, we must first listen. When what others reflect to us embodies the same conceptual model, we know that we've achieved a common understanding.

Listening is not something we do only when someone else is talking. If your architecture teams work with engineering, product management, or other teams that write their own designs, specifications, and other documents, then listening to what those teams have to say requires reviewing their documentation. Note that this process involves reviewing—not just reading. It's all too easy to read a document without understanding it. If you're not tempted to leave a comment or two as you go, you may not be listening carefully enough to what the document has to say.

This does not mean that every architect should read every document produced by every other team. Most of the time, that would be impractical. Just as creating and governing a system's design is a team effort, so is managing inbound communication from your counterparts. It's helpful to document who's *expected* to read a given document and who *has* read it. Here again, good information architecture will help organize documents as well as make their status and relevance clear.

If your team sets a good example with its communication efforts, you may find other teams adopt similar practices. They might use similar templates, organize information in similar ways, or contribute definitions to a dictionary. If you see your best practices being copied in this way, take the time to encourage it. A simple benefit is that alignment of process and structure provides a broader foundation for common understanding.

A second benefit occurs when teams borrow and then improve on each other's practices. If another team adopts your template and then modifies it, look at what they've changed. Perhaps they've found a way to improve the template that applies to what you do as well. Taking the time to look at these changes, think about them, and apply lessons learned are all forms of listening to your colleagues. Everyone will benefit from sharing these improvements, and it will help create a strong work environment, too.

The best outcomes occur when disciplines merge their communication structures. That doesn't mean architectural documents and requirements documents will become one and the same; we need to keep the steps of the process separate. But conceptual models, information architecture, names—these are aspects of products, or even product families, and are not specific to software architecture. If you can align these across functions, then you've built the strongest possible common foundation from which to expand common understanding to new work.

Good communication also requires humility. Quite naturally, we take pride in our work. After explaining our work to others, regardless of the medium, it can be easy to confuse listening to confirm understanding with listening for acknowledgment. We all want our work to be acknowledged, but acknowledgment doesn't necessarily reflect understanding.

Conversely, understanding is acknowledgment—even if it doesn't feel that way. Perhaps you've had the experience of someone explaining your work to you when they don't realize you're already familiar with it and have never spoken to you about it before. At first, this might be frustrating because there's no *explicit* acknowledgment of your contribution.

But what an amazing moment that is! Someone you haven't spoken to on the subject has reflected your own thinking so clearly that you can recognize it as your own work. Without a doubt, that demonstrates effective communication. Far better to revel quietly in the accomplishment of the work and its communication than to worry about who's getting credit.

Summary

Developing a product is a team effort, and no team can function without effective communication. The most productive teams operate from a shared conceptual model of what they're building. They use both written and verbal communication to establish, maintain, and evolve that understanding.

Communication should place a heavy emphasis on written documentation. Writing facilitates collaboration across locations and time zones, is persistent and scalable, and forces clarity of thought. Use documents to capture information that would otherwise be hidden or lost in emails or chat messages.

Complement writing by creating time and space for your team to talk. Longer, in-person meetings are especially helpful when establishing new concepts and in building team rapport. Ad hoc conversations can help resolve misunderstandings or other concerns. Having a regularly scheduled time for these engagements, such as a team meeting, can provide a backstop for smaller topics, as well as maintain team connections over time.

Projects generate a lot of documentation. Invest in an information architecture that will let everyone—not just architects—find the documentation they need. Make communication a conduit for feedback that will improve your work.

When communicating, pick names carefully, sticking to clear, descriptive names and naming patterns. Document the names and use them consistently. Maintain a project dictionary that captures these names, as well as other important terms used by the project. These efforts will help improve your own clarity of thought, as well as facilitate communication with the broader team.

All teams spend time and energy on communication. With a structured approach to documentation, information architecture, and naming, teams will find that those investments help them work productively and efficiently.

Chapter 9

The Architecture
Team

This book is about building an effective software architecture practice within a software development organization. Software architects, and the team or teams into which they are organized, "own" that practice, in the sense that they define, evolve, and maintain an architecture. These architects also own the processes via which the team operates: how work is tracked, change proposals are developed and reviewed, decisions are made, and communication is undertaken. The team may be deliberate and intentional in these actions or simply ad hoc. Either way, they set the documented or de facto processes by which the architecture works.

The size, operation, and formality of these teams vary greatly from one organization to the next. Four people in a garage coding the next great product need software architecture, but they don't need to create an architecture team, specialized roles, or complex decision-making processes. They can probably consider the entire company—all four of them—to be the architecture team. (They may also be the product management team, the engineering team, the testing team, the operations team, and the sales team.) Decision making and communication can be as simple as taking off their headphones for a moment for a brief check-in with the rest of the crew.

In larger organizations, hundreds or thousands of individuals may work on a single product. Even larger efforts, spanning related product portfolios, may involve tens of thousands. To scale up, organizations first apply specialization, creating smaller teams focused on specific disciplines. Then, they stitch these back together through structure, processes, and tools that provide the necessary coordination. For large efforts, the organizational know-how this work requires can itself be both a challenge and a competitive advantage.

Having discussed how a software architecture practice should operate, we now turn to how it should be structured as a discrete discipline within a larger organization. Just as there is no one perfect organizational structure, there is no best or single model for the architecture team. There are, however, a set of common concerns that every organization should consider in this regard.

Specialization

A good place to start is with the question of whether architecture ought to be a specialized role within an organization. While I firmly believe that architectural skills are a prerequisite for building great software, organizations have a continuum of options as to how they label, recognize, and integrate that skill.

At one extreme, "software architect" can be a discrete role, and the people occupying this role are expected to specialize in the subject. That is, they are hired for their expertise with and knowledge of software architecture; they are expected to continue to grow and refine their knowledge of the subject; and, within reason, they will not be asked to take on other tasks.

At the other extreme, an organization might consider all software engineering roles to require a mix of skills. In these organizations, software architecture isn't a specialization, but rather one of many skills that everyone is expected to have and apply. They might also be expected to have skills and knowledge for mobile application development, cloud computing, and databases.

Both approaches have their benefits and drawbacks. The challenge with the generalist model is that these individuals can't be competitive, in every part of their job, with specialists in those same areas. Indeed, that's one of the reasons that specialists exist: to create the space to acquire and apply a deeper understanding.

To borrow an example from outside the software realm, consider who does the accounting for the four-person start-up mentioned earlier in this chapter. Is each of the four coders expected to also maintain the accounts for the business? That's not impossible, but it's also not likely. These individuals may be generalists when it comes to software, but software itself is a specialized field. They'd probably rather hire an accountant than tackle that part of the job.

Similarly, within the software arena, there are many areas of specialization: mobile, web, services, databases, search, security, machine learning, and so on. Architecture is simply one more subject on this list. Ultimately, each team should consider, for each of these areas, whether they need a specialist. Which specialists are worth investing in will vary based on the size of the team, the product domain, and other factors.

Taking these considerations into account, the need for and value of specialization tends to be driven by two factors. First is scale. As discussed earlier, the larger the project and the larger the organization, the more value that exists in organizing around specific functions. For every project, there is a tipping point at which architecture is a full-time job for no other reason than the amount of architectural work that's required. Once you reach this stage, adopting a specialist-based approach will, if done properly, be more effective than continuing to disperse responsibility.

The second factor has to do with the product's starting point. Not all products break new ground with respect to software design. If you're building yet another iteration of a well-established architecture, using tried-and-tested technology, then even a large project may not involve much architectural work. In that case, you might not need architecture specialists. For example, consider a team building a new variation of an existing game. Tweaks to gameplay and updated content will make the new game fresh. New architecture work probably isn't needed and would only serve to make the project more expensive.

In contrast, some products demand new architectural thinking. For example, when smartphones were first introduced, no one really knew how best to architect a smartphone application. Architectures for desktop applications were a poor fit because they made assumptions about the life cycle of the application that use on mobile devices invalidated. Conversely, leveraging architectures for applications developed on the much more limited phones that had come before the smartphone also didn't work well, because they accommodated limitations that no longer existed with respect to, for example, user interaction models.

The level of specialization required is, therefore, a function of the project and its circumstances. On the one hand, there's no need to have a dedicated architecture team for projects that don't warrant significant architectural efforts. On the other hand, if you're venturing into new territory due to shifts in technology or platforms, significant architectural work is likely required. In that case, creating specialized architecture roles will help the project succeed.

Structure

Assume that a development organization has created specialized architecture roles. Again, that choice may have been made because the team is large and has many specialized roles. Or the system may be architecturally challenging, a challenge that can be addressed by hiring relevant expertise. Whatever the motivation, how should the architecture team be structured, and where should it be placed within the larger organization?

As with specialization, there's no one answer, but rather a continuum of choices. At one end is a centralized architecture team, separated from other functions. At the other end is an architecture team that is entirely "virtual," with each architect reporting into a (probably cross-functional) team. The best point on this continuum for your team can be found by considering various factors.

One key factor is organizational size. In smaller organizations, the virtual team tends to work more smoothly, for a couple of reasons. Notably, there tends to be less need for specialization in such organizations. A centralized architecture team encourages its members to do nothing but architecture. If you want architects to tackle a mixed bag of tasks, it's better to embed them in the team that shares those responsibilities. The organization structure should reinforce responsibilities, not work counter to it.

Centralized architecture teams also create their own overhead. They'll need a manager, for example. The manager might themselves be an architect, but once the team is established, they'll inevitably spend some time on non-architectural management tasks. In a small organization, it may be possible to collapse all of that back into the managers of smaller, cross-functional teams and eliminate the need for an additional position. In a larger organization, centralizing the architects might offer valuable relief for overloaded managers elsewhere.

A potential downside of distributing your architects throughout the organization is that it may be more difficult for them to communicate and organize among themselves. Architecturally related, cross-team tasks will tend to be perceived as secondary to their own teams' goals. Of course, for small teams, or products without significant architectural challenges, this may not be an issue.

Should the lack of crosstalk among architects become an issue, various structures can be overlaid to balance these concerns. The simplest way to create this structure is often as a *virtual team* to which the architects also belong. While virtual, such a team will still need—at least to some degree—a process, communication, meetings, planning, and so on. Without some structure, nothing will be accomplished.

If you're using a virtual team model but architectural work is not running smoothly, then it may be time to adopt a more centralized model. Many organizations do well with a *hybrid model*, in which the organization maintains both a centralized architecture team and architectural roles on multidisciplinary teams. A significant advantage of this approach is that it creates a space within the central team for the larger, cross-cutting concerns that need attention but can be difficult for any individual architect to find time to address on their own.

Another advantage of the hybrid model is that it can elevate architecture's voice in the organization. When architects are embedded in multidisciplinary teams, their voices are filtered individually through the leaders for those organizations—and this has the effect of diluting them. The point here is not that anyone is deliberately quieting them but rather that such dilution is an inevitable effect of this style of organization.

With a *centralized* architecture team, the leader of that team can instead represent architecture in leadership discussions. In part, this helps give architecture a clearer, more consistent voice. For example, the architecture leader might note that several engineering teams are tackling similar design challenges in an uncoordinated way and can suggest shifting to an aligned architectural approach.

Perhaps even more importantly, an architectural leader is responsible for sharing and explaining leadership decisions to the architects. In this way, the centralized architecture function, despite being a separate team, can help cut *against* isolated architectural thinking. The lead architect takes on the responsibility of creating strong alignment between the organization's goals and architecture's activities.

At the other end of this continuum of choices lies the fully centralized architecture team. Perhaps the biggest advantage to this approach is that it helps scale the architectural function, making it straightforward to provide administrative and program management support. As with any team, such support can help keep work on track—and even accelerate it. A centralized, consolidated team also helps architects coordinate and speak with one voice, which can be especially valuable on projects that are working with new and evolving architectures.

Figure 9.1 illustrates these three ways to structure the architectural function within a product development organization.

To summarize:

- In the centralized model, all architects report to a single leader, who in turn reports to the organizational leader. This creates stronger connections within the architecture team, but looser links to engineering and other functions.

- In the virtual model, none of the architects reports directly to the architecture leader—if there is one. Instead, they report to leaders elsewhere in the organization. The architecture leader, if present, maintains a looser, "dotted line" relationship with them.
- The hybrid model combines the other two approaches, with some architects reporting directly to the architecture leader, and others remaining in the engineering teams.

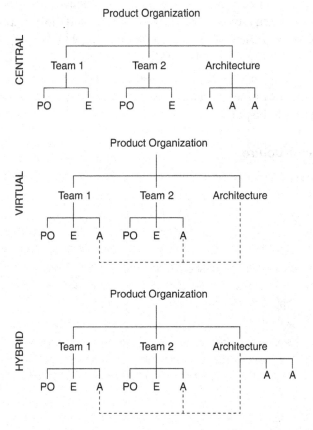

Figure 9.1
Three ways to structure the architectural function within a product development organization. Here the PO, E, and A labels indicate individuals in the product owner, engineer, and architect roles, respectively. These roles vary in title and number at different organizations.

Organizations vary widely in how they are structured, so for purposes of illustration, the other teams have been shown somewhat vaguely in Figure 9.1. Meanwhile, team members are identified as "product owners," "engineers," and "architects." However, many other structures are possible, not all organizations have product owners, and so on. The structures illustrated in Figure 9.1 should be reinterpreted in the context of your organization, rather than taken as prescriptive.

No matter which model is chosen from this spectrum of options, maintaining alignment and communication with engineering and other teams is essential for success. When architects belong to a central team, communication among themselves is in some sense easy, as many factors promote ongoing conversations within a team. Leaders must then take extra care to create communication channels between architects, engineers, and others.

With the hybrid model, there is the additional risk of creating a division between architects on the central team and those embedded in the engineering teams. This risk can be mitigated by keeping the centralized team relatively small and always including some of the product architects in its meetings, communications, and so on. In other words, the boundaries of a central architecture team, especially in a hybrid model, should be porous.

Substructure

Some systems are too large to be served by a single architecture team, regardless of how it is structured. An architecture team that includes more than a dozen or so people is likely too large to be manageable. Whatever the exact limit for team membership, once it is exceeded, consider delegating responsibility to "sub-teams" that focus on specific areas.

Sub-team assignments should align with the decomposition of your system. For example, a sub-team might be responsible for the architecture of a subsystem, service, or application. As noted in Chapter 5, it's ideal to have your organizational structure match your system structure.

When sub-teams have clear assignments, it's also easier to determine which changes are their responsibility. If a change impacts only components and relationships within their assignment, then it's theirs to manage.

However, if a change impacts additional components or relationships, it should be raised to the main architecture team—avoid having two sub-teams work directly on such changes. The problem with the one-to-one approach is that it gives the two sub-teams a strong incentive to make narrow changes without impacting the rest of the system. Although we don't want any change to have a broader impact than necessary, we do want to identify changes that apply systemically and address them accordingly. That, of course, is the role of the main architecture team.

Leadership

Team structure must also consider leaders—both the ones you have and the ones you want to have. You'll have little success with a centralized architecture team if you don't have someone capable of leading it. Conversely, a strong architecture leader without a supporting organizational structure will likely be more frustrated than productive.

As discussed earlier, some projects don't require strong architectural leadership. Generally, that's because they're not breaking new ground with regard to software architecture. For such teams, there's no more need for a strong architecture leader than there is for a centralized architecture team. Such cases exist but are not our focus here.

Projects with virtual architecture teams require a leader who is comfortable working across team boundaries. Many senior architects, having developed a point of view on how they want to see architecture run, are good candidates for this role. As they have no direct reports, they needn't take direct management responsibility for anyone, which may be an advantage in recruiting them for the role. Nonetheless, they will need to coordinate with the architects' direct managers on each of the teams from which they are drawn.

To shift to a hybrid or centralized model, you'll need an architecture leader who can take on direct management responsibilities. Architecture leaders capable of handling these responsibilities may find that it simplifies their job, insofar as they do not need to coordinate with another manager who may establish different goals, provide different feedback, and so on.

For larger organizations, some hierarchy will be necessary. Although it is possible to create an architecture team with its own structure, consideration should be given to using a hybrid model to help address issues of scale. That is, keep the central architecture team small enough to be run by a single manager, and keep additional architects embedded in engineering teams. Whereas creating a separate hierarchy tends to undermine the partnership with engineering, hybrid models reinforce it. And partnership is essential to seeing designs through to successful implementation and operation.

When using a hybrid model, consider de-emphasizing the organizational boundaries and referring, instead, to all architects as part of a common "council" or the like. When using the hybrid model, from an organizational standpoint, some architects are on the central architecture team and others are not. That can make the architects who are not on the central team feel excluded—which is certainly not the intent—and undermine incentives for the two groups to work together. You can counteract these tendencies, as well as emphasize the need for all architects to work together, by adopting a different label, such as "council," that emphasizes their unity.

At the same time, councils should not fall into the trap of acting as inspectors rather than architects. A centralized council that simply reviews architectural work done by others isn't doing architecture. That doesn't mean there's no role for review, but better review practices have been covered earlier in this book. A centralized review function tends to create bottlenecks and disagreements far more often than it contributes to improved architecture.

Leading architecture at this scale, whether structured as a centralized or hybrid team, requires architectural, management, and leadership skills. Such roles are typically titled Chief Architect, Head of Architecture, or the like. The individuals filling this role should be considered part of the leadership team for the product, representing architectural concerns in concert with their counterparts in engineering, product management, and so on.

The remainder of this chapter addresses specific concerns and practices that help form and maintain high-functioning architecture teams. If you've hired a Chief Architect, these concerns are all within their remit. If these concerns are as yet unaddressed in your organization, it may be time to hire someone for this role.

Responsibility

Wherever you've placed your architects, specialization comes with its own risks. If a specialist is too divorced from other considerations, they may develop solutions that are impractical for the problem at hand. If you've hired a database specialist and they want to design a new database system from scratch, that's okay if that new database is your product; otherwise, it's probably a poor choice for your team.

A subtler form of this problem occurs when architects produce reasonable work but fail to take responsibility for its completion. This frequently takes the form of an architect who completes a detailed design for some change and then simply walks away from it, failing to work with the engineering and operations teams who will shepherd that change through realization.

No matter the form it takes, ignoring reality seems to be a risk for architects, so much so that these "ivory-tower architects" have been given their own moniker. And really, there's nothing valuable in an architecture practice that is divorced from the reality of product development. The time and effort spent on designs that are never implemented—or worse, are discarded during development because they don't work—are a drain on the entire organization's resources.

To counteract this risk, architects must be held responsible for the implementation and operationalization of their work. Delivery of a detailed design is not the end of their work on that change, but rather the end of the beginning. A change is not done—and certainly not successful—until sometime after it has shipped and is demonstrably meeting its original goals and requirements.

An excellent way to emphasize responsibility is to track these stages as part of the change process. Recalling the backlog discussed in Chapter 7, "implementation" and "operation" can be made additional states through which each item is tracked. Rather than closing an item out when the change is done, keep it open until the change has an operational track record. Until then, the responsible architect cannot consider the change to be complete.

If you adopt this approach on an existing project, the architects involved may find this new responsibility jarring. That's a strong indicator that they previously viewed their responsibility as ending when the detailed design was complete. You will see improved results by changing expectations and asking them to stay engaged throughout the entire process. However, don't forget that this will require time and effort for which they had not previously accounted. You may need to reduce their load of new architecture work accordingly.

Again, while change proposals remain in one of these two additional states, architects remain responsible for checking in with their counterparts in engineering and operations. Possibly it will all go smoothly, but it's likely that something new will be learned. Is the change proving difficult or expensive to implement? Perhaps adjustments can be made, or lessons learned for the next change. Does the change match the operational expectations for performance, scale, and cost? Perhaps further work is required to tune the system.

When issues arise, the response must be disciplined, not ad hoc. Keeping architects engaged throughout the process is not an invitation to short-circuit the discipline of your change process. If a change is not working, fixes should not be made willy-nilly. Rather, new change proposals should be developed, vetted, and run through the process—always. They may be small changes and they may have associated urgency, so prioritizing them may be warranted. Still, following the process will help avoid poor decisions, backtracking, and confusion.

Your architectural design process should take this need into account. When discussing velocity (in Chapter 7), I mentioned that data from one project showed a typical design took 4 to 6 weeks. If each change always took 4 to 6 weeks, however, we would not have been able to maintain any semblance of process discipline and still ship anything on time. When issues arise during implementation, it must be possible to address them more quickly. On that project, the same process could turn around a small change in as little as a day but still without cutting corners.

As a final step, consider documenting lessons learned from the implementation and operationalization of these changes. While likely not worthwhile for every change, this is an especially valuable practice for large, significant changes. As noted earlier, writing down these learnings will make them accessible to the largest possible audience.

Ultimately, the best way to address the risks of specialization is not to avoid it, but rather to emphasize that an architecture practice—as with all aspects of product development—exists to serve product delivery, and not the other way around. If you find yourself with architects who act as if the product is a playground for their architectural thinking, they have misunderstood their role.

Talent

Whether your architecture team is small or large, hybrid or virtual, its success depends on the talent and skills of its members. Identifying and developing architectural talent is thus a critical activity. This should be part of the job description for anyone running a central architecture team. (With a hybrid team, this person's remit should be all architectural talent in the organization—not just those on the team.) If architects are embedded in smaller teams, then this responsibility may need to be assigned to a more senior architect, or perhaps a member of the organization's leadership team.

No matter how your architecture practice is organized, explicitly acknowledging this practice and how it operates helps create an associated career path for individuals within the organization. They may use this knowledge to identify architecture as an area of interest and take their own actions to pursue it. Alternatively, it may provide a helpful starting point for conversations with individuals who want to advance their career but aren't quite sure how to go about it.

An architecture career track is ideally positioned as one of several options. That's the point of specialization, after all: It's a choice among options. Individuals who prefer to pursue graphics or databases or other topics will, ideally, see those as equally viable options. The point here is not that each specialization is on equal footing, but that the best results arise from aligning individuals' talents and interests with the organization's needs. Conversely, a bad outcome is one in which individuals specialize in architecture because they see it as the best, or even only, opportunity to advance their career path.

Presumably your employer has a human resources team; look for ways to partner with them. Many manage programs designed to identify and nurture talent. Architects, and the architect career track, should be as much a part of this discussion as, say, management talent.

A mentoring program can also help identify and nurture talent. As a bonus, it often provides benefits to the mentor as well as the mentee. Mentoring programs need not be formal, although they certainly can be. For any program it's necessary to make it clear that architects are expected to spend some amount of their time on mentoring, and everyone can benefit from being a mentee.

Architects should also encourage and model continuous learning. So much of what we know about how to do our job isn't learned at school, but rather over years and decades of experience in the field. Some experienced practitioners have taken the time and effort to share what they know by writing books on the subject. Any architect not taking advantage of such a simple, inexpensive way to boost their own knowledge by reading those books is missing an enormous opportunity.

As valuable as talent is in becoming good at something—software architecture or anything else—it must be coupled with a willingness to work hard for real success. In identifying and developing talent in an organization, look for individuals who are eager to learn from mentors, books, and other resources in addition to their own experience.

Diversity

A strong team—architecture or otherwise—contains a diversity of views and experiences. In Chapter 4, we discussed the value in developing a variety of approaches to each potential change—in the form of change proposals—before committing to one direction. That's one example, but certainly not the only one, where diversity drives better results.

Unlike in nature, diversity in organizations does not seem to arise as a matter of course. On the contrary, human biases tend to result in uniformity. When hiring architects, we quite naturally tend to favor candidates who "look like architects." And if architects are doing the hiring, that can mean we too easily favor those who look like ourselves.

Unfortunately, this is not a process that can be addressed simply by improving hiring practices. Indeed, for certain roles, even recruiting a diverse set of candidates can be difficult. It is not easy to hire someone for a role when they haven't applied.

Developing a diverse software architecture function therefore requires playing the long game. Take diversity into account when recruiting, interviewing, and hiring. Take it into account when identifying and developing talent, as discussed in the previous section. And look for ways to encourage those with the skills and interest to enter the field by making it a welcome place.

Regardless of the makeup of your current team, remember that inclusivity allows diversity to thrive. A diverse team will do little good if its members don't feel comfortable contributing—including sometimes challenging the status quo. Many of the practices discussed in Chapter 7 are structured to promote inclusivity by creating different modes in which anyone can participate.

Culture

Once the connections between architects in your organization start to gel—whether in a virtual, hybrid, or centralized model—they'll develop a team culture. Norms will be adopted. Some of these will be minor. Perhaps, are emojis acceptable in emails?

Many of these norms will form around more significant topics. Architecture leaders have a responsibility and an opportunity to steer these behaviors toward those that best serve the product development organization. Ideally, action is taken before negative behaviors take hold and cause trouble.

Team culture is a broad topic, and we've already touched on specific elements. For example, "work in the open"—discussed in Chapter 4—is in part a cultural norm. So is adherence to the practices laid out in Chapter 7: Does the team take them seriously, or is it okay to ignore them when they seem inconvenient? And creating an inclusive environment, as discussed in the previous section, is very much an aspect of a team's culture, too.

Beyond these and other examples in the book, I've collected here five other aspects of team culture that I have found to be the most important and most worthwhile to actively cultivate.

- **Teamwork:** We've been using the word "team" extensively, so it might seem odd to think of teamwork as requiring special emphasis. And yet, it's all too easy for a "team"—especially when it's virtual or hybrid—to be nothing more than a group of people working together. The distinction is in how they operate: Are they on their own, or do they provide each other with encouragement and support?

  When you've built a strong culture of teamwork, no one goes it alone. Working on a tough problem? Others will chip in. Need to step away from work for an hour, a day, or a week? Someone will cover for you. Need a review of a document you just wrote? A teammate will make time to review it. In a group that's not yet a team, everyone has an individual sense of responsibility. Teams take on a sense of shared responsibility and then the members work together to meet it. They succeed or fail collectively, not individually.

- **Humility:** No one has all the answers and gets everything right. When someone challenges your ideas or catches your mistakes, they're not finding fault with you—they're helping you do better. And the same goes for the team: Teams, too, can make mistakes and must have the humility to accept them, correct them, and move forward. To do so, we must have the humility to know that we can always learn more and do better.

- **Partnership:** As noted repeatedly, software architecture exists to serve the larger goal of developing great products. It is not a means unto itself and should not be undertaken in pursuit of its own glory. Success requires a strong partnership with everyone else involved in creating and delivering a product—which is often a good many people. Chapter 10 explores this topic in more detail.

- **Customer focus:** The teams that produce the best products never forget that they cannot succeed if the product doesn't work for the customer. And what the customer requires is not always best served by the most interesting, most innovative design—or the cheapest and easiest. Customer focus also helps maintain a sense of urgency: Customers care not only about solutions to their problems, but also when those solutions arrive.

- **Rigor:** Architectural work involves many steps: documenting the current system, developing change proposals, decision making, communication, and coordination. There's a lot to do and often limited time in which to do it. It can be tempting to cut corners. Over time, that leads to incomplete and inaccurate documentation, which leads to poor decisions, which leads to mistakes and then failures.

  Teams can best counter this dynamic by demanding rigor at every step of the process. If that's new to a team's practices, it will feel slow at first, because each step will take longer. Over time, however, it helps teams work faster. They'll have better, more accurate information to hand. Decisions will be better, and fewer of them will be changed later. And the resulting product will be better, too.

These and other elements of team culture should reinforce each other. Teams with strong positive cultures produce the best work, and they do so predictably. They're also the most satisfying to be a part of.

Gathering

In my experience, few things help transform a group into a team more than time spent together—and doubly so for time spent together over a meal. I don't claim to know why that works; I expect it's some deeply human phenomenon. If it works, it works.

As a bonus, much of an architecture team's work can be accelerated by spending some time together in a less formal setting. (The importance of conversation as part of communication was covered in Chapter 8.) Forming a team takes time, and eating a meal together takes time, and conversations take time.

Add all of these points up, and you have a strong argument for gathering your team together physically. This practice is especially valuable when forming a new team, but I recommend making it a regular practice even for long-standing teams. Even if you can gather only once or twice a year, it will make a difference. Meet for at least a few days, or perhaps a week.

The topics in these gatherings will naturally evolve over time. Perhaps your first meeting—or two or three—will focus on developing shared concepts and terminology. At some point, that will be done. But these concepts are rarely static: Products grow and evolve, and they'll require changes. Any sizable project will always have new topics to discuss in these regular forums.

If your team is distributed, people will have to travel to attend. That's great, because asking participants to make time to travel and step away from their day-to-day concerns helps bring their focus to the conversations that happen at the meeting. You're asking everyone to be present for these conversations not just physically but also mentally.

If your team is co-located, consider changing the venue to emphasize this same physical separation and mental focus. Perhaps you can choose a different but nearby location. Even a conference room in your office that you don't normally use will do; it helps if it's on a different floor or the next building over.

Seminars and Summits

The previous section addressed gathering on the scale of individual architecture teams, which may be all that your organization requires. Bigger organizations, with multiple architecture teams, will want to consider some additions to these get-togethers.

A seminar series provides a good, albeit casual, mechanism for creating cross-team communication and collaboration. A seminar series might be held anywhere from once a week to once a month. Generally, an hour will suffice. Presenters can primarily come from the teams themselves, although the occasional guest speaker might be warranted.

Seminars should be interactive, as creating space for conversation is most of what fosters cross-team connections. Thus, presenters should not bring so much material that they entirely fill the allotted time. If they can be recorded, those recordings can serve as a useful complement to the system's other documentation.

Just as it is productive to get individual teams together in person periodically, so it is with larger meetings for multiple teams. A multi-team summit will require substantial time and attention, plus potentially significant expenses. Once or twice a year is probably the right cadence for such a get-together.

A strong summit agenda will cover two to three days. It will focus on topics that are broadly applicable to the audience; this is not the time to "go deep" on narrow concerns. (Separate meetings can be held for those.) It will also build in time for networking over meals, during long breaks, and at the end of the day.

Summary

There are many ways to structure an architecture practice within a product development organization. The best fit for your organization will depend on factors such as the size of the team and the nature of the project. Teams can be structured as virtual, hybrid, or centralized. Organizations should pick the model that best fits their concerns and needs.

Regardless of the organizational structure selected, strive to knit your architects together into a team. When they're brought together into a team, the support they provide for each other will help them to do their best work. Strong architecture teams take responsibility for their work throughout implementation and operations. In this way, the architecture team, even if virtual, becomes a strong partner for these other functions.

Nurturing an architecture team takes efforts familiar to any manager. Talent must be identified and developed. Diversity can bring value to any team and helps support strong change practices. A team culture that emphasizes teamwork, humility, partnership, customer focus, and rigor will keep everyone pointed in the right direction.

Teams are further supported by making space for ongoing conversation. These spaces can include in-person gatherings, topical conversations, and ongoing check-ins that maintain space for important but not urgent discussions. In larger organizations, seminars and summits that cross product boundaries can help create an architecture community.

The role of Chief Architect encompasses the set of architectural, management, and leadership skills required to run a successful architecture team. The larger the project, the more critical this role becomes in developing an effective software architecture practice.

Chapter 10

The Product Team

Imagine creating a new software product as a solo pursuit. First, you will have to wear a product management hat, working to understand your customer, describe a market need, and begin to define your product. Next, you will probably want to spend some time with both your architect and user experience designer hats on, as you work through identifying the concepts that animate your product, organizing the software components, designing a corresponding user interface, and so on. Once your designs are far enough along, you can switch to engineering and write code, then to testing for verification. Along the way you will likely spend some time on project management concerns— even if you are just managing your own time. Later, once the product is released, some time will be allocated for operational concerns, customer feedback, marketing, and sales.

That's a lot of hats to wear, which is why it's no surprise that few software products are solo pursuits. As teams grow, roles are specialized. While there is no precise cutoff, by the time a team contains dozens of members, it's likely that product management, program management, user experience design, architecture, engineering, testing, and operations are each handled by individuals with specialized training and experience in those roles.

Thus, software architecture is not practiced in isolation; it's a specialized role among many, each necessary to bring a product vision to fruition. The need to build and maintain connections between your architecture practice and the broader product organization has been mentioned many times as we've examined the internal workings of that practice. Now, we turn our attention once more to how architecture works with, supports, and learns from the other specializations involved in software product development.

The roles, responsibilities, and labels used for these specializations vary between organizations. That's a natural consequence of a variety of factors, including organization size, industry, company culture, and ever-evolving thinking on how best to structure such organizations. Therefore, the categorization used here probably doesn't exactly match that in your organization. And if you work in one of these other disciplines, you may be especially aware that your view of your work doesn't fully align with the description here. Please know that the structure selected here exists primarily to guide the discussion; it is not intended to be prescriptive with regard to how these roles should be labeled, or even how software product development organizations should be structured.

Working with Development Methodologies

Any project of nontrivial size will adopt a methodology to organize the process of software development. There are dozens of such models: agile, spiral, the Rational Unified Process, and so on. More than anything, this plethora of approaches makes it clear that no one approach works well for all organizations and all products.

Methodologies organize how and when work is done, but they do not fundamentally alter what work needs to be done. For example, no methodology dispenses with the need for user experience design. Methodologies might prescribe when that design should happen, whether it's (nominally) a one-time occurrence or iterative, how the design work is prioritized, and so on. Still, the design is necessary, and it must be done; no methodology can change that.

Similarly, while different methodologies have very different points of view on how and when architectural work is to be done, none can obviate its need. We have, therefore, been able to discuss software architecture—what it is, the context in which it operates, how to manage change, how to make decisions, and more—without resorting to any specific methodology.

Furthermore, teams inevitably adapt, modify, and refine methodologies to fit their needs. Even the methodologies themselves evolve, as new approaches gain currency and old ones fade away. To make the practice of software architecture contingent on a specific methodology would be to make it both irrelevant and obsolete at a stroke. Architecture—like user experience design—is a discipline that each methodology must account for, and not the other way around.

Nonetheless, to create an effective architecture practice, you will need to align your architecture practices with the product's development methodology, whatever it might be. Consider those practices in two parts: one part that depends on the methodology at hand, and one that does not.

The methodology-independent half includes the architectural principles, vision documents, and system documentation. These activities should be undertaken regardless of which methodology is used because they're foundational to architectural work. If they do line up with some aspect of the organization's methodology, that's okay, too. For example, many organizations incorporate an annual planning cadence, which is an excellent time to update your vision.

In the methodology-dependent half are the change proposals. Recall that change proposals represent an increment of work, taking the system from its current state to some future state. That doesn't change based on methodology; what does change is when you develop change proposals and how you scope them.

For example, consider a methodology that emphasizes completing the design work before implementation begins. That's simply another way of saying that change proposals should be developed and completed during the design stage. Because you're doing all design up front, you'll likely have quite a few proposals to develop, and those may be substantial in scope. The architecture team will be quite busy during this time, but nothing about the approach changes the need for design.

Conversely, a methodology that emphasizes just-in-time design might pick up much smaller change proposals for each iteration. Here the value in developing principles and vision really comes to the fore, as they help drive alignment across these many smaller increments. Without such forcing functions, there is a real risk that many smaller designs might work against each other, rather than reinforcing each other.

One of the powers of the change proposal–based approach is that it scales between these two extremes. With this approach, you needn't make fundamental changes to your architectural process as development methodologies change or evolve. Architectural work is still architectural work, after all.

It's also helpful because you may find that, in practice, you'll need to adapt. Suppose you are using a design-upfront approach and later, during implementation, discover a defect in the design. You cannot return the entire project to the design phase, but you can do some just-in-time design work. Flexibility helps.

Conversely, handling too many, small, just-in-time proposals can be more difficult than dealing with somewhat larger proposals that take on a more natural scope. Thus, even when you're using a highly iterative methodology, some change proposals may naturally evolve to larger increments.

Ultimately, the architecture process should support the organization's methodology, not drive it. At the same time, those adaptations should not undermine the team's ability to do architecture well.

Working with Product Management

An architect needs two things from their product manager. First is a set of capabilities and requirements that describe what to build next. Second is the planned trajectory of those capabilities over time.

A *capability* is anything the product does, expressed from the customer's point of view. Capabilities often correspond to features and functions. For example, word processors have a *print capability*. When invoked, that capability triggers selecting a printer, formatting the document for the printer, generating the print stream, sending it to the printer, and so on. If you're building a word processor, your product manager will want to include a *print capability*.

Capabilities are not always features and functions. They may correspond to "nonfunctional" requirements, which are generally concerned with performance and other dependability considerations. For example, perhaps your word processor can already print—but only documents with 100 or fewer pages. In this scenario, printing much larger documents—say, 10,000 pages—can be reasonably described as a new capability. Indeed, challenges in scaling up, such as printing ever-larger documents, often require substantial architecture work.

Capabilities are described as a set of requirements. Just like the designs, specifications, and other artifacts produced by architecture, they should always be written down. Documents—preferably based on a template—provide for capturing details and support asynchronous reviews that other forms of communication, including presentations and discussions, don't accommodate.

Requirements explain what a capability must do and, at least implicitly, what it need not do. Continuing the example, a printing capability might be described with requirements such as these:

- The application MUST allow the user to print the current document to any available printer using the system print settings and dialog.
- The application MUST allow the user, when printing a document, to apply a "DRAFT" watermark to the output.

Just these two requirements tell us, as an architect, quite a bit about what we'll need to design for. For example, it's clear that we shouldn't invest in a proprietary print dialog or connectivity. That might be appropriate for some applications, but here the requirements clearly and usefully state that our application will leverage print capabilities from the underlying operating system. Without doubt, that is an architecturally significant requirement.

For all these two requirements do say, they nonetheless omit requirements related to performance and scale. That's an oversight. You might think that such requirements could be reasonably inferred—after all, who hasn't used a printer?—but, in practice, such assumptions lead to trouble. As an architect, you might think that printing a page per second is entirely reasonable. Your product manager may know that your customers have high-speed printers running a hundred times faster.

As an architect, it's not your job to infer these missing or implicit requirements. However, it is essential to look for them. Experienced architects often develop a knack for spotting these gaps and asking product managers to fill them in. As you review the requirements, ask yourself if they address throughput, latency, scale, efficiency, and so on. These mental checklists will necessarily vary by domain; think about what matters for your work and strive to identify the gaps. If possible, work with your product management team to add these items to their requirements template.

Also think ahead to potential changes. Capabilities don't always require changes: Sometimes the current design can accommodate them, even if some new code is required. Or, the design might require some enhancement, but within the bounds of the current architecture. These are ideal outcomes, indicating that the system's current architecture is well aligned with its evolving capabilities, and allowing for the least expensive implementations.

When new work is required, and especially if architectural changes might be needed, look for requirements that give you the freedom to explore two or more approaches. Product managers will sometimes author requirements to telegraph an intended approach. Architects sometimes encourage this tendency by sharing, early in the process, the changes they're considering. If everyone seems already aligned, writing requirements that assume or imply an implementation may seem simple and expedient.

Avoid this trap and push back on overly prescriptive requirements. The most obvious problem that can arise occurs when you change your mind. After all, you only shared your initial thinking; once you see the full requirements and have more time to think things over, you might well decide to take another approach. Evaluating alternatives is, after all, part of the job.

It's problematic, though, if the requirements telegraph one implementation and you elect to proceed with another. Now your implementation won't address the requirements as written, although it may well meet the requirements as intended. It's that gap between the two that's an issue, and the only way to avoid it is to create requirements devoid of implementation assumptions.

Worse, that gap may hide significant assumptions and misunderstandings. For example, suppose your product manager has written requirements for a *save as PDF* capability. Your initial thought might be to leverage your *print* capability. After all, the PDF captures a representation of the printed page; both require the same layout work. Hearing this, a product manager might be tempted to require that *save as PDF* be implemented as a type of printer.

A PDF, though, is more than ink on a page. As an electronic document, it can be encrypted, contain live form fields, and so on. Great features, but irrelevant on the printed page, and not something your printing code will address. Does that mean supporting these PDF features is not a requirement? Or did your product manager assume these features could be added later?

These problems arise when requirements specify *how* something should be done instead of *what* should be done. When requirements don't give you the freedom to select from different design approaches, they've likely fallen into this trap. Even if you do plan to use the implementation they telegraph, push back. As you recast requirements to focus on what needs to be done, you may uncover new requirements or considerations that affect your design.

When reviewing requirements, you should also ask how you—and your product managers—will know if the requirement has been fulfilled. Ideally, requirements will be written as specific, testable assertions. For example, compare these two different approaches to describing a *save as PDF* capability:

- The application MUST allow a user to save a document as a PDF.

That's a testable statement—either the application allows this, or it doesn't. But it's less than specific. A product manager may end up with a less-capable capability than expected.

As an architect, you should work to draw out any hidden assumptions early so that you can account for them. Your product manager might have meant to write something closer to this:

- The application MUST allow a user to save a document as a PDF.
- When saving a document as a PDF, the application MUST offer the option to protect the document with password-based encryption.
- When saving a document as a PDF, the application MUST offer the option to convert all form fields in the document to fillable PDF form fields.

Or maybe not—possibly only the simpler version is required. Either way, it's essential to know. The simpler version (no encryption, no live form fields) is simpler and faster to create, and you shouldn't invest in building capabilities that aren't wanted. In contrast, if the additional features are required, then your design will need to account for these options. The need to map from your document's concept of a form field to PDF form fields may prompt you to rethink your approach to better align the two implementations of this concept.

Helping Out

We've discussed at length what architecture requires of product management, but as in any good relationship, information should flow in both directions. Product managers work a complex calculus to balance customer requests, their own sense of product and market directions, corporate strategic imperatives, schedules, deadlines, and so on.

As an architect, you can help. You can provide insights into which new features or capabilities might be accomplished easily, and which might take more effort. Letting product managers know which capabilities have a long lead time—because they require extensive design work or significant system changes, for example—is especially valuable. Lead time and level of effort are two important inputs for the product manager's calculus.

More helpful still is to establish a common language and understanding of the concepts your system realizes. Concepts (introduced in Chapter 2) provide the ideal level of abstraction for discussing what a system does without getting bogged down in the details of how it does it. Discussing a system in terms of concepts thus creates the same separation discussed earlier regarding requirements. That is, it preserves the architect's ability to change or replace a design without disrupting the capability that the design delivers.

For example, suppose that your product manager wants to add "save as PDF" to your application. They're aware of the similarities with printing and want to ship the feature quickly. The application can already print, they note, so surely adding "save as PDF" can be done quickly?

Concepts provide a mechanism to tease out and discuss the latent assumptions behind this question. The application already has a *printing* concept. If "save as PDF" is an aspect of the *printing* concept, then it will be relatively straightforward to add—but also limited by the scope of the print capability itself. *Printing* doesn't address encryption and form fields, so a "save as PDF" feature based on that capability won't address those either.

Possibly, your product manager would prefer to add a new concept. That could be a *save as PDF* concept. Such a concept would encompass PDF-specific features in its conception. It would be related to the print concept and might even leverage some of the same code, but it wouldn't be the same.

Or, perhaps "save as PDF" is only the first feature in a *format transformation* concept. Working with this broader concept, we can consider additional output formats, such as HTML. Such a concept would also have to generalize the notion of format features: PDFs can be encrypted but HTML cannot, yet both can support live form fields. Such a concept would model these similarities and differences.

To make this work, shift the conversation with product management from features to concepts. With a shared understanding of concepts, product managers can reason more accurately and more independently about the cost of addressing new requirements. That also ties the conversation back to the capability trajectory (discussed in Chapter 3) that architecture needs.

Other Outcomes

Not every engagement with product management results in a change to the system. Sometimes that simply isn't necessary; some requirements are simple enough that they can be handled within the boundaries of an existing design. If that's the case, chalk it up as a success and move on to your next challenge.

Sometimes, the process of reviewing the requirements and mapping them to concepts, capabilities, and features will result in extended discussions that result in the requirements being dropped entirely. That, too, can be considered a successful outcome.

Such an outcome typically occurs in one of two ways. The first occurs when the review reveals a lack of clarity on the requirements. For example, perhaps the differentiation between "print as PDF" and "save as PDF" hadn't been considered when the requirement was originally drafted. The ensuing discussion helps tease out the difference between the concepts. Determining which is desired might require revisiting the use cases.

After such a review, perhaps the product manager determined that "print as PDF" addresses the use cases. There's no need to support additional PDF capabilities. At this point, it may also be clear that the built-in "print to PDF" capabilities of the underlying operating system are sufficient. The requirement can be withdrawn, and no further work is necessary. That's a highly successful outcome, preserving precious architecture and engineering time for other work.

The second outcome occurs when it's determined that the return on investment is too small. Considering now the counterexample, assume that the clarified requirements indicate that "save as PDF" is the desired capability. Furthermore, implementing that capability will require modifying the application's document model because, while it contains form fields, its current model cannot support translation to PDF.

That can be changed, of course—but now the scope of the change has expanded from something limited to the printing subsystem to something pervasive. Product management may reasonably decide, on that basis alone, that the feature is not worthwhile. Again, that's a successful outcome—even if no new feature is shipped.

Setting Boundaries

Although occasionally new requirements are easily addressed, most requirements imply work is needed, whether it focuses on architecture, design, or implementation. And product management is responsible for prioritizing and sequencing capabilities—and thus the prioritizing and sequencing of that work. Again, that's the core of their job: to know their customers and market well enough to make this determination.

Organizations sometimes confuse this aspect of the product management role with the prioritization and sequencing of all architectural and engineering work. That is, they give product management authority to determine when work that is not directly driven by requirements will occur.

That's a mistake to be avoided. When the architecture team offers up these decisions to product management, they are abrogating their own responsibility to determine whether such work should be done. And it's unfair to the product management team, which is poorly equipped to make such a determination.

When this behavior arises, it's a sign of dysfunction. It indicates that the architecture team wants to make some architectural or design changes but is aware that the return on investment is low or, perhaps, unclear. (Often, the proposed change involves adopting some new technology.) A hard-headed assessment would almost certainly decide against proceeding.

By involving product management, the architecture team may hope to bolster the argument for this change by getting product management aligned with their desired pathway. But again, this is unfair to product management. If the change addresses some existing requirements, then there's no need for further confirmation. If it doesn't—and it's really an architectural concern—then how could the product management team make this determination? The only reasonable answer, from a product management perspective, is "no."

The point here is not that the architecture team can't prioritize engineering work. On the contrary, it's necessary that they can. But when they do, they must be fully prepared to justify that work on architectural grounds alone. It should be one of several change proposals that were considered; the rationale for proceeding down this path should be clear.

Ultimately, decisions about introducing new components or leveraging existing ones, evolving the system's relationships or working with its current form—these are decisions for architects to take. Don't undermine the architecture role by refusing to take make them.

These decisions can be enormously difficult, but they are part of the job. If you're struggling with trade-offs, look to your peers and other resources to help. See Chapter 6 on the decision-making process for further ideas. You might make a poor decision—we all do from time to time—but you should still own it.

Working with User Experience

Your counterparts in user experience—sometimes also known as experience design—are key partners for the architecture team. Although user experience teams often present their work as pixel-perfect designs, the work that those designs represent reaches much deeper. Done properly, the user experience reflects and conveys the concepts that animate a system.

When a product's user experience correctly reflects its intrinsic concepts, users can build a correct—and therefore useful—mental model of the product. With an accurate mental model, users will find that a product behaves as expected. It will delight them by aligning with their expectations and avoid the inevitable frustration of a product that behaves in inexplicable ways.

Whether a product delights its users depends only partially on whether it does something useful. That's a necessary condition, but not sufficient. If users have the wrong idea about how a product works, they'll struggle to use it all—no matter how well it might work.

To achieve a delightful product, then, requires a user experience that accurately conveys the product's intrinsic concepts. That, in turn, requires that the user experience team and the architecture team are aligned on those concepts.

It might be tempting here to think that architecture ought, by right, to establish the system concepts, with the user experience team then being charged with conveying these concepts accurately. Such an attitude, however, doesn't bode well for establishing a partnership.

At any rate, a conceptual model that can't be explained, or doesn't make sense, to your user experience team won't get far. And if your user experience team doesn't understand it, what makes you think your users will?

Far better to use your partnership with the user experience team to align on a conceptual model that everyone agrees is fit for purpose. Product management should be included in this conversation as well, as a good conceptual model is one that passes a three-part test:

- It satisfies the requirements as established by product management.
- It can be realized in the system's architecture with a reasonable design.
- It can be conveyed to users via some straightforward user experience.

Ultimately, arguments over ownership become immaterial when product, experience, and architecture align on these core concepts.

Working with Program Management

Your program management team is responsible for coordinating the work items that go into each release: assignments, dependencies, progress, and so on. Only a fraction of these work items will be architectural tasks, of course.

You can help program management by bringing clarity about when architectural work is required and when it's not. That can be an area of some ambiguity. A truly significant change to a product might require a change to its architecture. More frequently, only new design work within the confines of the current architecture will be required. Sometimes not even design work is required, if the current design is capable of handling whatever new features are required.

Those distinctions may be much clearer to you than to your program management team. Providing unambiguous insight into these distinctions, as early as possible, will help them map out not only the amount of work required, but also its scope and scale.

For these exchanges to be effective, program management will need to understand the different modes in which the architecture team can engage. If your team has not previously followed a rigorous architecture practice, you may find it worthwhile to invest in explaining these distinctions and processes to your program managers.

The architecture team can also help program management do its coordination work—and thereby help projects run on time—by formulating, describing, and making visible the design process. For example:

- If you work in the open, then program managers can easily inspect which designs have been started and which have not.
- If you use a standard design template, program managers can easily inspect, for a design in progress, which sections of the template have been completed and which have not.

- If you make clear ownership and approval assignments, program managers know who they need to check with when clarifying status and plans.

In an effective partnership with program management, the mechanisms via which architectural work are accomplished allow for a division of responsibility between *what* needs to be done, as determined by the architecture team, and *when* it needs to be done, as determined by program management. As an added benefit, all of that can help keep you and your team out of the business of program management and focused on the architectural work itself.

Program management is also necessarily concerned with managing dependencies between work items. Here, you should watch for incorrect or overly strict rules. For example, more than once I've seen architects who didn't want to review requirements until they were done, and engineers who didn't want to review designs until they were done. In other words, they were implying "finish-to-start" dependencies between the prior task and the next one.

That behavior reflects a misunderstanding of how the work is done. In general, each earlier task cannot be considered complete until its consumers—architects for requirements, engineers for change proposals—agree that it is done. And the best way for the consumer to make this determination is to have already started on the next task! As an architect, I can't really be certain that requirements are complete until I've produced at least a complete draft of my change proposal. Similarly, I cannot know that my change proposal is complete until engineering has given it a thorough review.

The correct dependency between these tasks is, therefore, "finish-to-finish": The next task cannot be completed before the prior task completes. However, the next task can—and indeed must—be started long before the prior task is done.

Program management is also a resource when planning and scheduling architectural work. Especially on large and complex projects, you will need to juggle a variety of tasks of varying scope and priority. If your program management team is asking for commitments to various dates, you're having the wrong conversation; you've taken on too much of the scheduling yourself.

Instead, work in the open. With your process as a reference, enumerate the work that needs to be done and estimate its scope. Then, partner with your program management team to construct a plan that appropriately balances and schedules that work. You may find that a design with a June commitment isn't needed until August because engineering is busy until then, or that it can't be started until August because the requirements won't be ready. By shifting the conversation away from dates and to the plan, you can enlist the program management team to help discover, untangle, and make the best of these situations.

Working with Engineering

Your elegant architecture and beautiful designs won't see the light of day until they are realized by your engineering team, which makes your relationship with that engineering team essential to your success. You should engage with them before, during, and after each iteration of the change process.

Begin by grounding yourself in knowledge of the current implementation. If you're new to a project, track down the source code repository and start reading. Your goal here isn't to read every line of code, but rather to gain a basic familiarity with the shape of the implementation.

Even a basic familiarity with the structure and quality of the code will give you critical information. For example, suppose you are reviewing code in a client application that invokes various HTTP APIs. That will not be a surprise in a system that leverages web architecture to communicate between clients and services. Maybe the architecture team designed the API, or at least established the standard to which the API was designed.

Even so, the engineering team will have made decisions—some critical—about how to implement those calls. Are they using the platform (i.e., operating system) HTTP library, or does the application include its own? Is the HTTP library multi-threaded or event-driven?

Can it stream large requests and responses, or does it hold them entirely in memory?

Many of these questions don't have right and wrong answers. Familiarizing yourself with the implementation is not the same as critiquing it—although it's probably inevitable that some critiquing will happen along the way. Still, for many applications, these implementation details are not critical, and nearly any approach will do.

Sometimes, though, they are critical. If your application is sending or receiving images via those calls, an in-memory implementation for request and response handling is not ideal and will not scale to larger image sizes. If that isn't an issue now, you can file it away as something to revisit later.

Often such considerations aren't an issue yet but will surface as problems later because of another change. For example, perhaps your application works well enough with images today, but product management wants to add video support in the next release. Supporting videos will substantially increase the size of the API payloads you're working with.

Ultimately, familiarizing yourself with the current system is about awareness. Usually, the current implementation isn't wrong. It probably meets all current functional and performance requirements. If it didn't, those would have been identified as defects, and the team would be working to address them.

Nor is it necessarily fair to say that every implementation needs to handle every eventuality. In fact, quite the contrary. Using a stream-based HTTP processing library adds complexity and might have slowed getting the first release out the door. Keeping your implementation as simple as possible for the current release has real value and is often the best strategy. If you can't get the image handling version out the door, you may never have the chance to add video support later.

Again, your goal here is to be aware of these limitations so that you can plan for them. When new requirements are evaluated, you should be familiar enough with the implementation to know which ones are straightforward—because the current implementation can address them with only modest changes—and which ones will require more extensive reworking of the code.

Is maintaining this awareness engineering's responsibility? It is, and it would be unreasonable to suggest that the architecture team is solely responsible for it. On the other hand, both you and your engineering team will find it tedious if architecture keeps making assumptions about how the code is written and engineering is forever disabusing them of their incorrect notions. If you're familiar with the code, you'll share a ground truth from which you and engineering can both work.

When you're working on a new change proposal, invite the engineering team to participate. Assuming you work in the open, this can happen naturally: You'll start a new change proposal document, engineering will notice the creation of the draft document, and they'll have a look if they're interested. You might receive comments before you're ready for them, but this level of engagement is undoubtedly a positive sign. At the same time, working in the open is not an excuse to avoid explicit communication. If you are working on a change proposal that you know you need to engage engineering on, be sure to bring it to their attention.

As the engineering team engages with a change proposal, program management may also be looking at them to provide some initial estimates. Estimation and work breakdowns are an excellent perspective from which to drive a review. First, they force thoroughness: Engineers will want to review every aspect of the change to produce complete estimates. Second, estimates provide a checksum for engineering. If the engineering cost for a change doesn't match the architect's ballpark expectation—based on their knowledge of the current implementation—then the estimate has raised a red flag and the gap should be investigated further.

Sometimes that gap arises due to miscommunication. No matter how clear we try to make our writing, engineering may interpret the document differently. If that's the case, a conversation with engineering should surface the misunderstanding. Sort it out—and update the document.

A deeper concern arises when the change has been understood but the estimates of work involved nonetheless differ. When this occurs, dig deeper—it often indicates a gap in the architect's understanding of the system. Possibly, the change is sound, and the higher estimates will have to be accepted.

Often, with a better understanding of the system's current state, changes can be designed so as to reduce the implementation cost. But that isn't an invitation to cut corners! Most requirements can be addressed via a variety of approaches. As we work, we are constantly trading off between many important considerations, of which the cost is certainly one. We're not looking here for cost savings that hinder our ability to achieve functional or nonfunctional requirements. Rather, we're looking for alternatives that are generally equivalent, yet with lower costs given the system at hand. These considerations are one reason a strong architectural process develops competing conceptual approaches before committing to one of them.

Following Through

Your engagement with engineering doesn't end when a change proposal is approved. It is critical for architects to stay involved with their work through the complete implementation phase and into use or production of the product.

The architecture team owes this engagement to the engineering team if you are to live up to your half of the partnership. Questions about the change will inevitably arise as the work proceeds, and the architects should be there to address them. Don't forget that each question is also feedback. These questions often arise when the details of a change were unclear or underspecified. The immediate concern should be addressed and, when possible, a lesson learned for the next iteration.

Speaking of iterations, avoid the temptation to modify a change proposal after its approval. To be clear, further changes may well be required. The detailed design might contain an error. A better approach might be proposed late in the process yet deserve consideration. It's even possible that requirements will be revised, requiring the planned change to be reconsidered.

Whatever prompts the need for change, remember that changes are handled via the change process. That is, rather than modifying the approved change, start a new one that encapsulates the new set of changes. As described in Chapter 4, you'll find that adhering to this practice helps immensely in keeping everyone aligned and reducing thrashing.

As you monitor the implementation, you may also identify changes that you want to make. These changes aren't necessary for the current set of requirements, but might be opportunities to simplify the system, improve dependability, add new capabilities, and so on. Capture these ideas in your backlog so they don't get lost, even if they are not all destined to be implemented.

Must Architects Write Code?

On small teams, with less differentiation between roles, architects might also be responsible for implementing in code (at least portions of) their own change proposals. There's nothing wrong with that, and indeed, small teams demand flexibility in roles and responsibilities.

Larger teams will sometimes debate whether architects "should" or "must" code. The implication here is that, if they don't code, they can't produce credible designs and engineering need not listen to them.

This is a specious argument that misunderstands the value of specialization. We don't require that architects also be product managers, or that all engineers also be architects, or that graphics engineers also be able to optimize SQL queries. There's no reason that the connection between coding and architectural credibility should be any more real than any other combination of skills mismatched to role.

Furthermore, architecture and coding are both demanding intellectual activities. By asking anyone consistently and constantly to do both, we are ultimately failing to recognize the effort required to do either one well. After all, that they are distinct and difficult is why the specialized roles have developed in the first place.

It is, of course, important for any well-functioning team that individuals in different roles respect and appreciate what others are bringing to the table. In that spirit, it's important that architects and other engineers, as with any other two roles, establish credibility and trust with each other. And if the way to do that—for some architect on some team—is to write some code, so be it. But we should equally not imagine that the ability to write code will somehow replace the hard work of collaborating as a team.

Working with Testing

Ideally, your project will have a team dedicated to testing, validation, quality control, and quality assurance—the general pursuit of ensuring that the software operates as intended, whatever name it goes by. Here we'll call that *testing*, with no disrespect intended to those who prefer a different label.

A comprehensive testing function validates the product at multiple points. Beginning at the end, tests validate that a product's capabilities and features operate as expected—that is, they do not contain defects that result in failures. Invoking an API should, for example, result in the system performing the documented actions for that API. It should not result in other actions, incorrect outputs, or kernel panics.

A comprehensive testing function will also evaluate the system's ability not only against basic functional requirements but also against dependability requirements. The specification for an API should describe not just what it does but also its scaling (how many simultaneous requests), performance (response time), resiliency (for example, due to hardware failures), and so on. These are all testable properties.

And a truly comprehensive testing function will validate that the system's capabilities address the requirements stated as inputs to the design. In other words, we want to know more than whether the API does what the API documentation states it does; we want to validate whether what the API does addresses the requirements that it was designed to address.

How testing accomplishes these goals is beyond the scope of this book. At a basic level, testing can be applied to any change to validate that it behaves correctly, meets the requirements, and so on. Nonetheless, there is much that architecture can do to assist with testing and validation.

Let's begin with documentation. That's often where testing teams begin, after all. Starting with the system specifications, they can identify testable assertions and, from there, develop test plans, scenarios, and so on to validate those assertions. The better the documentation, the more likely it becomes that those tests will themselves be valid and correct.

Good documentation does much more than describe what a system does. Good documentation also accurately describes and conveys the concepts that underlie the system, allowing the reader to develop an accurate mental model of how the system ought to work. When a tester has an accurate mental model, they can reason correctly about what the system ought to do—and ought not to do. Clearly, that's fundamental to creating correct and complete tests.

When you're writing documentation, try to consider the testers' point of view. Good documentation is always optimized for the reader, and your testers are some of your most critical readers. After reading your documentation, will they have enough information to validate the corresponding implementation?

If your testing team can be engaged early, then considering their point of view needn't be a theoretical exercise—you can simply invite them into the review process. Better yet, if you work in the open, they can invite themselves. Getting the testing team involved early is an excellent way to get testing done earlier, and thus to find defects (or just misunderstandings) earlier, when they are easier to fix.

When designing the system, also consider how your work will be tested. The general design challenge here is to make the system less of a black box while still preserving its integrity. The more thoroughly the internal state of a system can be inspected, the easier it is for testers to validate behaviors. Visibility also helps in the debugging process.

Most of the time, you will find that this goal aligns strongly with creating well-decomposed, loosely coupled designs. The key observation here is that when bindings between components are minimized, the connections between them become points of inspection, and then tests can be written against them.

Testing teams can take advantage of these connections in various ways. Again, the simplest option is to use them for inspection. Basic interfaces that provide read-only access to important attributes and state information all help testers to validate the state of the system as tests exercise its functionality.

Inspecting the intermediate system state is so valuable that many systems include logging functionality that, in effect, provides an always-on, read-only view of the system as it operates. Whether logging is appropriate depends on the system you are building. When it's appropriate, you should look at logs as part of the interface of the component that produces them. Although you don't need to document logging behaviors as strictly as, say, programmatic interfaces, documenting some basic expectations will allow the testing team to use log events more reliably as part of their validation process.

In more sophisticated approaches, connections can be used to interpose testing code. That code might simply monitor or log events and invocations. Or it might go further by changing behaviors between different components. This technique can be used to deliberately introduce faults into a system, thus allowing failure states to be synthesized and the components impacted by those states to be evaluated.

Such approaches are also closely related to creating test harnesses for either individual components or isolated subsets of components. These components expect to be integrated with other "real" components performing their standard duties. However, with sufficiently clear interface definitions and dynamic binding, it becomes possible for testing teams to create substitutes for certain components, which they can then use to create more-or-less arbitrary test conditions for other components. In fact, this is really the only way to test that a component is hardened against misbehaviors from other components on which it depends.

All of these techniques can be applied to any single design, but they become even more powerful when they are integrated into the architecture of the system. In effect, they become a standard part of each design. For example, if a system uses logging, it should do so with a level of consistency about what is logged, when, and to where. The testing team can then learn just once how logging works, and subsequently use that knowledge consistently across their validation efforts.

It is similarly helpful to standardize how different system elements bind to each other. That's why many architectures define a dynamic binding mechanism of some kind in which, during initialization, components look up their dependencies—perhaps in a registry or discovery service. Using a singular mechanism not only simplifies the system's architecture but also provides a unique control point from which testers can interpose their own logic for monitoring, fault injection, and so on.

Finally, testing provides a wealth of information that may inform your next design iteration. While produced late in the process for any given cycle, test data will typically highlight any aspects of the system that are particularly problematic. Metrics here vary, although the number of defects is perhaps most obvious. Ask for this information and use it to identify which portions of your system might require extra attention in future designs.

Working with Operations

Software products aren't done when they complete testing. In fact, it's better to think of testing as the end of the beginning. After that comes deployment and operations.

As with testing, deployment and operational requirements should be considered inputs to architectural work. Thus, the architecture team should engage with the operations team throughout the change process.

Not all changes will affect deployment and operations, of course. Generally speaking, any potential impact on deployment and operations can be determined at the conceptual stage. At that point, you're determining how you'll go about making the change, but you haven't yet worked out the details. That's the right time for a quick check-in with the deployment and operations teams. If there's no impact, they needn't spend more time on that change. If they are impacted, then they can be involved as the work progresses to the detailed stage. (Not all organizations maintain separate teams for these functions. If yours doesn't, look for individuals who fill these roles, whatever team they're on.)

Few systems define their own deployment and operations mechanisms. Many reside on platforms that include deployment capabilities. That might be an application store for applications, a container management system for cloud services, and so on. Further complicating things, some platforms support multiple deployment options. Mobile and desktop operating systems support deployment via application stores—and via enterprise software management tooling, sideloading, and more. Far better to support these than to reproduce them. Alternatively, you might be deploying software to bespoke devices, which won't have a deployment capability unless you build one. Or, you might be managing the deployment of services in a data center environment, where, while choices abound, you nonetheless need to choose. Whatever situation your system faces, your partners in deployment and operations likely have expertise in these systems and can help you make wise decisions.

Once deployment occurs, you'll need to deal with operations: monitoring the running software, detecting and recovering from failures, changing configurations, and so on. Again, a myriad of solutions applies for different types of devices at different points in the stack.

As you develop and evolve your architecture, you should engage with your operations team on all these topics. There's no right answer to dealing with these challenges. Moreover, as is typical of the software world, the technologies involved are changing rapidly. The aim here is not to provide advice on how to design for deployment and operations, but rather to emphasize that it's necessarily a joint effort.

That said, deployment touches on a critical architectural issue for most systems: New software versions are rarely deployed simultaneously to all devices. There's necessarily a roll-out over time, so that different versions will coexist at any given moment. In fact, many deployment strategies depend on the ability to roll out new versions gradually and, should a new issue arise, roll them back. Thus, not only are new versions deployed piecemeal but, in many systems, old versions can also be deployed over new versions.

In some controlled environments, some constraints can be placed on this problem. For example, you might decide that your services can only be upgraded. If a new version contains a defect, you can stop that roll-out and replace it with an even newer version, rather than rolling back. However, this option is not universally available.

When dealing with software deployed to client devices, it's impossible to avoid the installation of old software or dormant devices coming online while still running outdated versions. If you want to try an interesting experiment, turn off a laptop for a few months and then bring it back online. There's a good chance you'll have to wait through a few hours of updates before it's caught up with updates to the operating system and applications.

Furthermore, all systems maintain state. If they didn't, they'd have no memory, and they wouldn't be very useful. That state can take any number of forms: rows in a database, files, or even persisted only in in-memory records.

Wherever it is stored, state is persisted according to some rules. Generally, we call that a schema for a database and a format for a file, but the problem is the same: Persisted state has some form, and all versions of the software that read and write that state must agree on that form or things will break.

Thus, some architectures need to accommodate different deployed versions of the system reading and writing the same state. Newer versions of the software need to be able to read state data written by older versions—that much seems obvious. But unless you have unusual control over deployment, your design will also have to accommodate older versions reading data written by newer versions. And while making that intertwinement work can be hard, it is almost always easier than guaranteeing that no older version will ever read data written by some newer version.

Your deployment and operations teams will be on point to manage the complexity of these scenarios. They will be familiar with the capabilities of the platforms on which your system is deployed, as well as the capabilities of the system you've built. And when things go wrong, they'll often be on point to determine how to proceed: halt an update or proceed, roll back or stay the course. For all these reasons, they're critical partners for architecture teams.

Summary

Architecture is but one of many functions required to develop, ship, and operate a software product. A common understanding of how these functions work together, including what each offers to the other, is an essential aspect of creating a well-run product development organization.

Organizations operate according to some methodology, albeit to varying degrees of fidelity. These development methodologies vary widely in how they structure the development life cycle. Nonetheless, they all describe how work is organized, rather than prescribing which work is done. Thus, while architecture teams must adapt to various methodologies, the core work of developing principles and visions, documenting the system, and working incrementally to evolve the system doesn't change.

Establishing and maintaining working relationships with product management, user experience, program management, engineering, testing, and operations are all part of the architecture team's remit. These functions provide inputs to architecture, and architecture provides inputs to them. As the one function charged with understanding how the entire system works, architecture has a big role to play in helping all functions work together.

Conclusion

As time passes, software grows ever more complex. We've grown accustomed to products that put the information and tools we want to use at our fingertips across multiple devices, anywhere on the globe, while supporting billions of users. Most of the time, they just work.

But if you've ever built one of these software systems, you know the enormity of the effort required. These systems are built by hundreds or thousands of people in efforts that span years or decades. They don't "just work"—they work thanks to massive, coordinated efforts over time.

How do you design such a system? Keep track of its components? Manage its evolution? These are the challenges that define software architecture as a discipline. It's architecture that gives us the processes, tools, and ways of working that manage this complexity.

And yet: Architecture isn't an inaccessible pursuit, available only to the priesthood and consisting of obscure rituals. At its core, practicing architecture requires straightforward, even unremarkable work. Effective software architecture requires a strong design process, but what engineering discipline doesn't? It benefits from effective decision making, but what job doesn't? Writing things down, defining terms—these are items of practical advice, not rocket science.

The good news, then, is that architecture is accessible to everyone. You might be thinking of establishing a new architecture function in your organization, wondering how to improve the functioning of the one you have, or anything in between. Whatever stage you're at, the straightforward, unremarkable guidance given here isn't out of reach for your organization.

The challenge is that even straightforward, unremarkable guidance can be difficult to put into practice. If the guidance given here was easy to follow and widespread in adoption—well, I wouldn't have written this book. This book was born out of a recognition that even organizations that want to do better may struggle to figure out what steps to take.

Much as I'd like it to be otherwise, I don't believe there's a simple practice-of-architecture playbook that can be applied to every organization. Every organization has its unique practices and challenges, not to mention its people and culture. If you want to transform the practice of architecture in your organization, mapping the guidance here to the specifics of your situation is, necessarily, an exercise for the reader.

Nonetheless, I'll close this book by offering some observations as to where you might start, what you might prioritize, and how you might "pick and choose" the best options for your organization.

Vision

Just as architects work toward a vision (see Chapter 4), so, too, can organizations. If you haven't already done so, consider developing—and writing down—a vision for the software architecture function in your organization. Like a technical vision, your organizational vision is intended to drive alignment and facilitate decision making.

As you develop this vision, you may find that you need to invest in explaining software architecture. That's an excellent opportunity to define software architecture as a discipline, describe how it operates, and explain how you see it helping your organization to succeed. You may find the discussion in Chapter 1 a helpful reference.

Architectural Recovery

If you don't have good documentation on the current state of your system, consider tackling this task early on. As explained in Chapter 4, a solid understanding of what you have now is essential to deciding what you plan to change.

As you document the system, you should capture several types of information. This is an excellent time to create a dictionary. Establishing common, clear, and concise definitions will be invaluable when you're recovering the designs of various system elements. As an added benefit, you may find that it clears up confusion in your day-to-day conversations, too.

Design documentation is, of course, the primary output of this exercise. If you run this exercise to completion, you should generate a set of design documents sufficient to describe the entire system: all its components, and all their relationships. That's not quite the system's architecture, but if you can take one more step and infer the implicit organization and underlying principles, then capture that, too.

Finally, while you're at it, use this opportunity to catalog the components you are documenting. Your software catalog is itself a valuable resource, and a good a place to which to link the design documents you've written.

Organizational Change

Establishing an effective architectural practice doesn't require organizational change. At the same time, organizational change is a tool that you can use to emphasize priorities, shift communication patterns, and garner attention. If you don't have an architectural team, consider forming one. (For more on structuring your architectural team, see Chapter 9.) If you don't have an architectural leader, consider creating the role and hiring one.

Once you have a team in place, take action to bring your architecture team together. Developing a set of architectural principles serves a dual purpose here: It brings the team together and produces an important input for further work. Other team-building activities will also work, of course.

The Change Process

For many organizations, governing change through a process and associated practices represents the biggest opportunity for improvement. The challenge here is, of course, that the team is already designing software and has existing practices in place. Improving those practices, even when the changes are welcomed, can be disruptive.

For these reasons, and in the spirit of working iteratively, I discourage you from making wholesale changes to the process. Instead, "pick and choose" from the ideas here. Bring in one change at a time, evaluate it, and then iterate.

If you don't maintain an architectural backlog, that's an excellent starting point. You'll find that such a backlog brings clarity to the entire process, and it's foundational for many of the practices described in Chapter 4. It also tends to be noncontroversial; it's difficult to argue against making a list and keeping track of things.

Another good starting point is adopting a change proposal template. Most architects will find this kind of template helpful because it makes their work easier, not harder.

Beyond these starting points, consider where you feel the most pain in your current process. If you can fix the parts that cause the most trouble—reviews or decision making, perhaps—you'll get the biggest return on your investment. Refining the process can be worthwhile, but be aware that further changes will yield diminishing returns.

Final Thoughts

The challenges involved in creating and operating software systems go far beyond those associated with the simple, stand-alone software products of just a few decades ago. While only one of the many disciplines that work together to conceive, realize, and run these massive systems, software architecture uniquely demands an ability to see the "big picture," to understand how all the elements of a system come together, and to evolve that structure over time. Over the last two decades or so, architects have made great strides in developing technologies and architectural styles that meet these challenges.

An effective software architecture practice is one that integrates this knowledge with the broader challenges of product development. Architects are perfectly positioned to aggregate requirements and, therefore, to design a cohesive whole instead of a collection of parts. And thanks to that same overarching view, they are well positioned to communicate to everyone how those pieces come together.

Doing that well requires more than a degree in computer science and more than experience with relevant architectural styles. It demands a predictable, repeatable process. The ability to make decisions expediently and effectively. A comprehensive, consistent, and clear communication strategy. Tools that promote efficiency. And a team that is greater than the sum of its parts.

Simply put, how an organization practices software architecture has an ever-increasing impact on its ability to develop and deliver fit-for-purpose software. These practices will help you lead your organization to a more effective practice of software architecture and to build better products faster.

References

1 ANSI/IEEE 1471-2000, *Recommended Practice for Architectural Description for Software-Intensive System* (2000).

2 Jackson, Daniel, *The Essence of Software* (2021).

3 Taylor, Richard, et al., *Software Architecture: Foundations, Theory, and Practice* (2010).

4 Bass, Len, et al., *Software Architecture in Practice* (2022).

5 Larman, Craig, and Victor R. Basili, "Iterative and Incremental Development: A Brief History." *Computer* (June 2003).

6 Parnas, D. L. "On the Criteria to Be Used in Decomposing Systems into Modules." *Communications of the ACM* 15 no. 12 (1972): 1053–1058.

7 Conway, Melvin. "How Do Committees Invent?" *Datamation* (1968).

8 Jansen, Anton, and Jan Bosch, "Software Architecture as a Set of Architectural Design Decisions." In *Proceedings of the 5th Working IEEE/IFIP Conference on Software Architecture* (2005).

9 Covey, Stephen, *The Seven Habits of Highly Effective People* (1989).

10 Norman, Don, *The Design of Everyday Things (2013)*.

Index

delegating, 107
dependencies, 99–100
engineering, 192–193
information gathering, 96–98
inputs, 95
keeping the status quo, 100–101
outputs, 95
principles, 11–13
product management, 187–188
responsibility, 106–107
right-versus-wrong framing, 104–105
stakeholders, 106–107
timeliness, 98–99
uncertainty, 105–106
decomposition, 81–82, 86–87. *See also*
components
delegating, decision making, 107
deliverable/delivery
discrete, 25–26
incremental, 50–52
single, 26
dependability, 19–21, 120
dependency/ies, 8, 97, 98–99
in decision making, 99–100
task, 191–192
deployment, software, 201–202
design, 75–76, 89. *See also* architecture
architectural evolution, 79–80
versus architecture, 13
composition, 82–85
concepts, 18
constraints, 12, 77–78
Conway's law, 87–88
decomposition, 81–82
engineering, 76–77
feedback, 88–91
incremental, 85–86
over time, 36
requirements, 40
starting over, 91–92
working in the open, 89–91
developer/development
accountability versus authority, 49
building a platform, 30–31
incremental delivery, 50–52
platform, 84–85
short-term approach, 46–48
talent, 169–170
velocity, 44
dictionaries, 150–152
discrete deliverables, 25–26
diversity, team, 170–171
document/s and documentation, 58–59, 60,
133–134. *See also* proposal
ADR (architectural decision record), 110
change proposal, 62–64
collaboration tools, 137–138
decision, 109–110
dictionaries, 150–152
implementation, 168–169
information architecture, 142–147
model, 186–187
PDF, 183–184
sharing, 139

status, 120, 125–127
summary, 120
templates, 119–122
updating, 60, 71–72, 146
vision, 61–62, 64
writing, 136–139, 197–198

E

edge, application, 25, 27
engineering
coding requirements, 196
decision making, 192–193
design, 76–77
involving in change proposals, 194–196
software
flexibility, 77–78
skills, 158
team, 192–195
environment, selecting, 29–30
estimates, 128–129, 194
evaluation, proposal, 70
evolution, 47
architectural, 52–55, 79–80
capability, 39–40
system, 14–16
technology, 53–54
experimentation, 79–80
external constraints, 3

F-G

feature, needless re-creation, 59–60. *See also*
concept/ual
feedback, 88, 89–91, 134
financial debt, 103
flexibility, software engineering, 77–78
formal standards, 32
fundamental organization, 2–3, 14–15
conflicting, 10–11
operating system, 9–10
future proofing, 44–45

H

"in house" standards, 32
HTTP, 33–34
human resources team, 169–170
humility, 172
hybrid team model, 161–162, 165–166

I

IEEE, definition of architecture, 2, 13
implementation, 17–18, 20, 21, 38, 59, 100,167,
193, 196. *See also* change/s
documenting, 168–169
MVC (model-view-controller) architecture, 25
standards, 32–33
important work, 71
incremental
delivery, 50–52
design, 85–86
information, 133. *See also* names